T0014492

RUBIK'S
TM

First published in Great Britain 2024 by Farshore
An imprint of HarperCollins*Publishers*
1 London Bridge Street, London SE1 9GF
www.farshore.co.uk

HarperCollins*Publishers*
Macken House, 39/40 Mayor Street Upper,
Dublin 1, D01 C9W8, Ireland

Written by Emily Stead

The Rubik's Cube facts stated are correct as of the time of going to print.
Best efforts have been made to ensure accuracy of content.

ISBN 978 0 00 861749 3
Printed and bound in the UK using 100% renewable electricity at CPI Group (UK) Ltd
001

A CIP catalogue record for this title is available from the British Library.

This book contains FSC™ certified paper and other controlled sources to ensure responsible forest management.

For more information visit: www.harpercollins.co.uk/green

RUBIK'S™
POCKET
PUZZLES

WELCOME TO THE WORLD OF RUBIK'S ... BUT NOT AS YOU KNOW IT!

The world's best-known puzzle, the Rubik's Cube, has challenged players since 1974 with every twist and turn. But if you've beaten the Cube, get set for a brand new way to play.

Challenge yourself with more than 70 puzzles and brain teasers in this book, inspired by the original Cube. Some are as easy as 1, 2, 3, while others will test your brain power to the max.

SO TURN THE PAGE AND DARE TO SOLVE!

LEVEL 1

CUBE COUNT

Wanna play? **Count the number of cubies** (single cubes) in the six groups below. Warning: there may be some cubies you can't see.

A

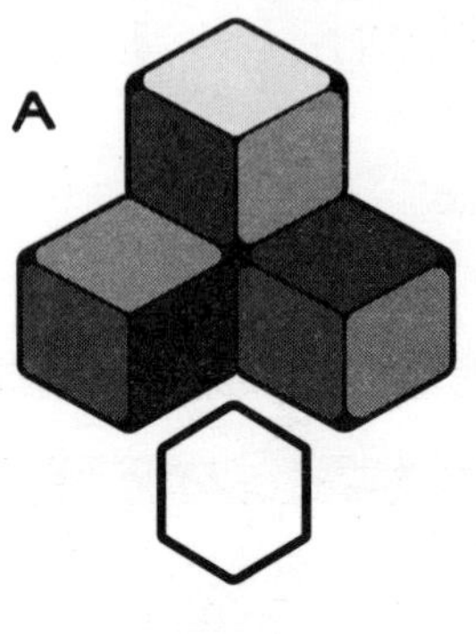

B

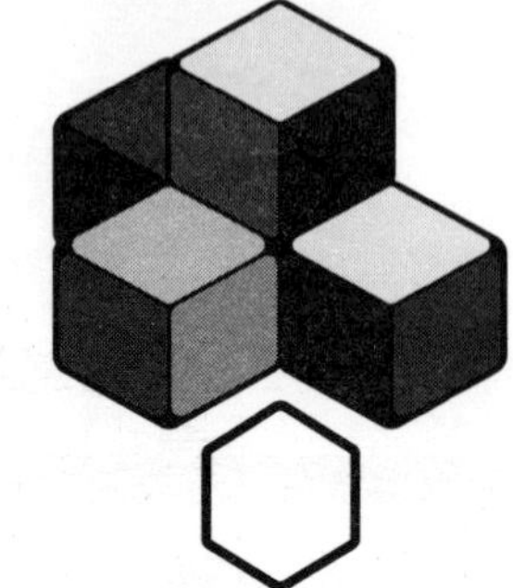

C

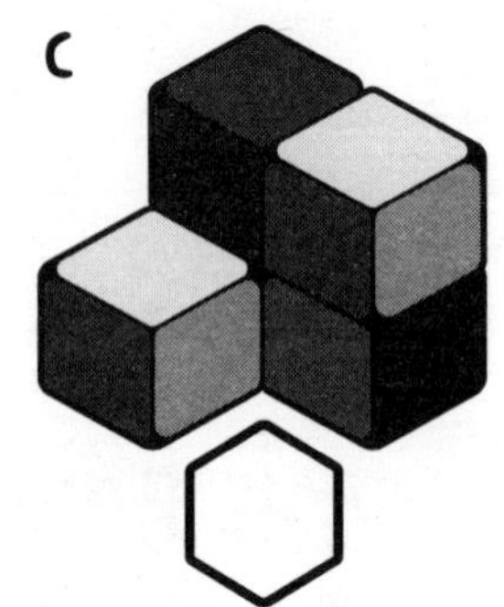

D

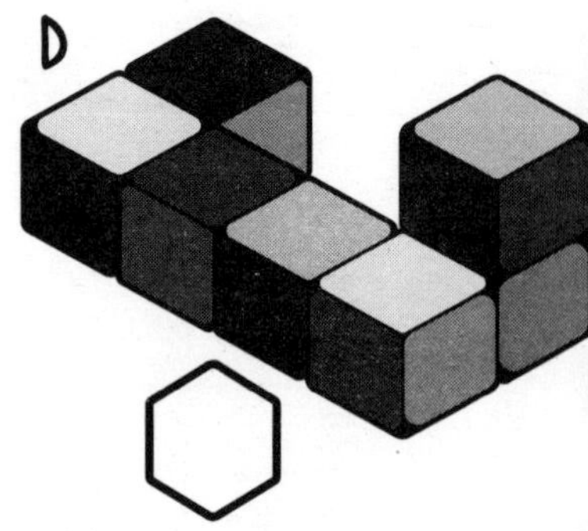

E

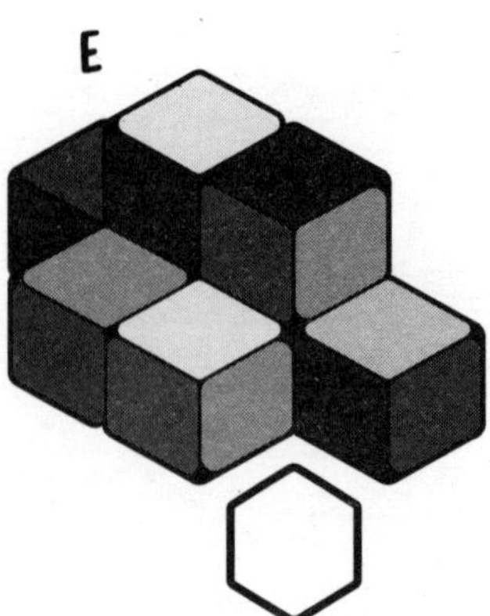

F

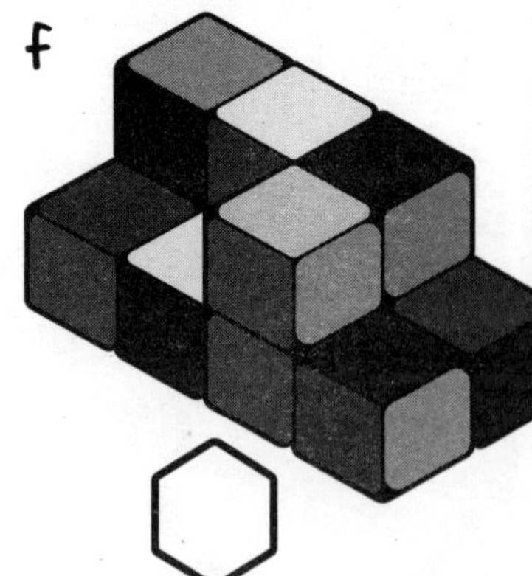

RUBIK'S LABYRINTH

Make it to the **centre of this labyrinth** where a precious prize awaits – a fresh new **Rubik's Cube.** Where to start, though? It's over to you.

LEVEL 1

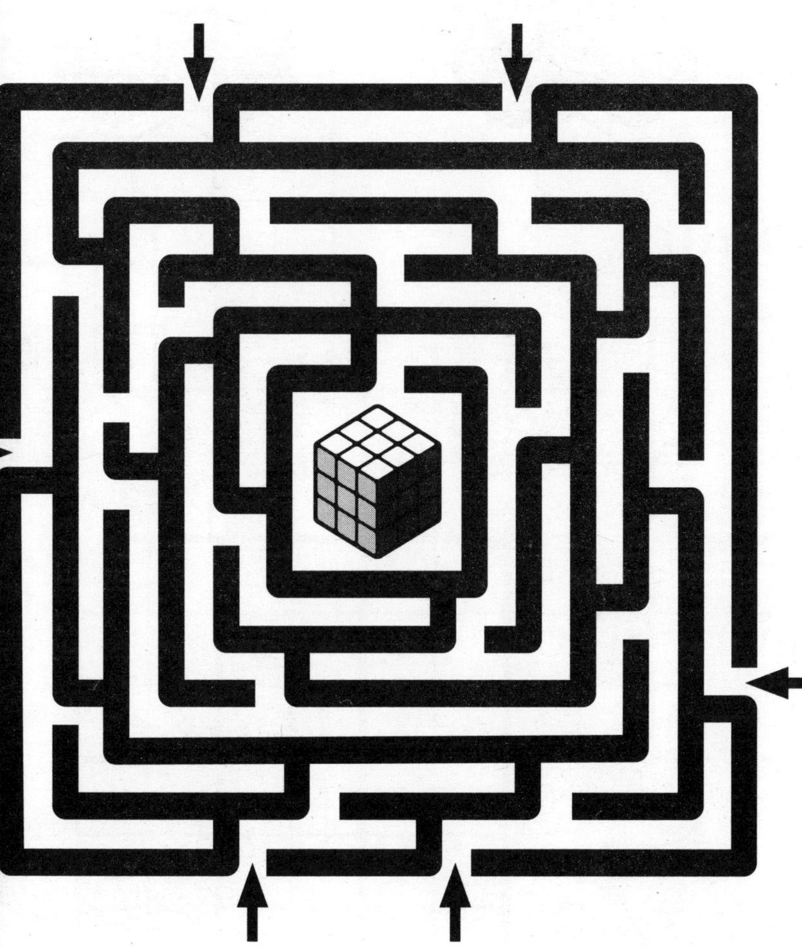

LEVEL 1

DOUBLE TROUBLE

Pit your wits against these gruelling grids! Complete the grids so that the **numbers 1 to 6 appear once only in each row, column and mini grid**. Puzzles 2 and 3 share the **central grid**. Tricky!

PUZZLE 1:
Easy

		5	3		1
	3	4			
	6			5	3
		1		6	
			5		
5		3	2		

PUZZLE 2:
Hard

	4		5		
6	2		3	1	
5				6	
	1		4	5	
		2			1
3				4	2

PUZZLE 3:
Hard

5					1
	1		6		5
4	2	5		3	
	3				4
	5	4		6	2
		6		1	

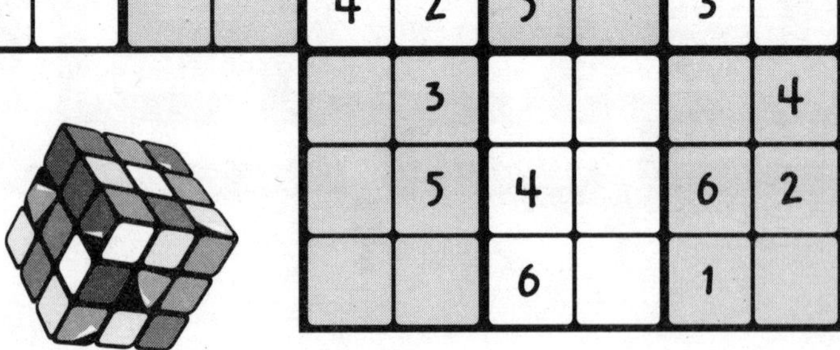

WHOSE CUBE?

Sure that's your Rubik's Cube? Then prove it! Change the word 'CUBE' to 'MINE' in just four steps. At each step, **change just one letter to make a new word, without rearranging any of the letters**. Start by changing the 'B' of 'CUBE' – use the clues to help you.

LEVEL 1

Clues:

Pretty or adorable.

Silent or no sound.

A tiny bug.

CUBE CONUNDRUM

Half the nets below transform into perfect cubes – can you work out which **three** they are? Try making the cubes using a piece of paper if you get stuck.

1

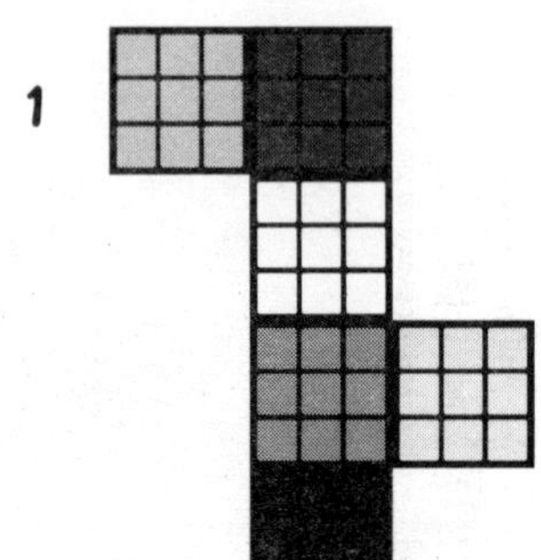

2

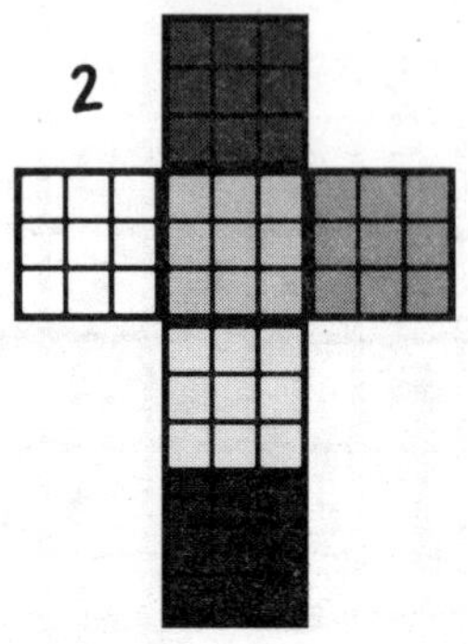

3

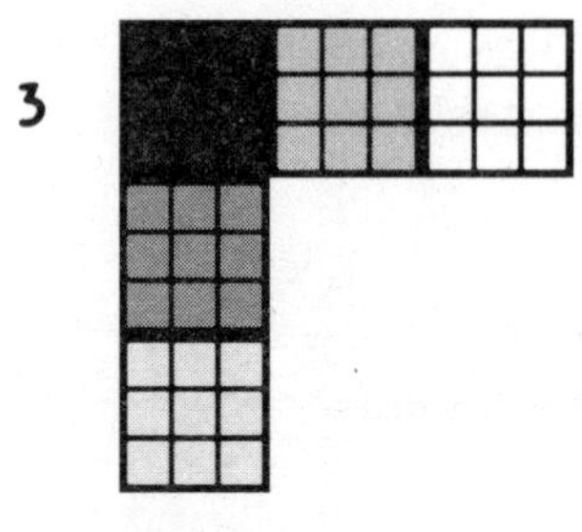

4

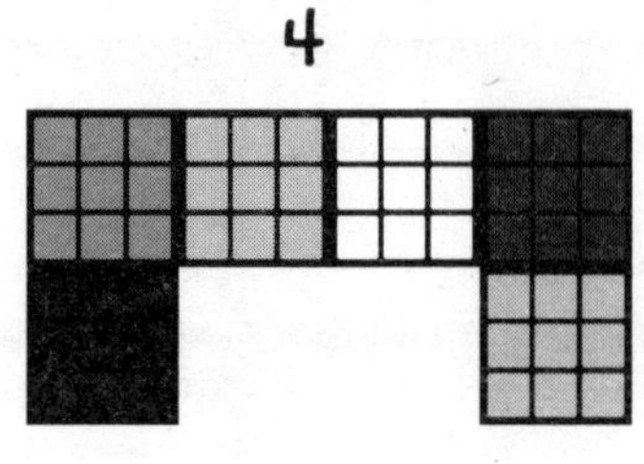

5

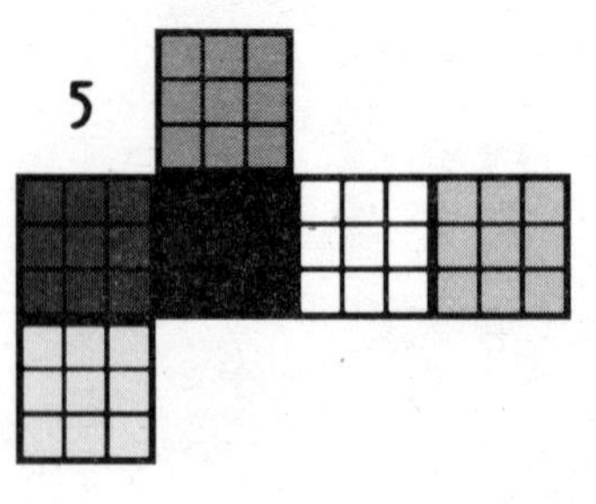

6

READY, SET, GO!

Starting at the **letter A** each time, cut a path through the grid in the **order of the alphabet**. You can **travel one square at a time** – forwards, backwards, up or down. Diagonal moves are **not allowed**!

LEVEL 1

1

START >		A	M	J	R	U
N	D	C	B	C	N	O	M
F	E	J	K	L	M	B	E
G	H	I	A	U	N	O	T
I	F	U	L	W	E	P	L
L	D	C	S	T	A	Q	D
P	J	G	D	T	S	R	O
U	Y	W	V	U	B	Z	S
S	T	X	Y	Z	> FINISH		

2

START >		A	B	E	F	G
G	E	L	C	C	D	G	I
H	F	I	D	L	E	H	X
I	D	P	M	U	F	I	J
J	G	H	B	K	Q	U	K
T	R	S	Y	O	N	M	L
C	X	N	Q	P	P	S	C
N	T	S	R	Y	Z	T	Y
M	U	V	W	X	∨ FINISH		

GRID GAMES

Complete the grids so that **everything adds up**. You'll need to work out some **subtraction puzzlers** too. Never accept the easy life!

PUZZLE 1

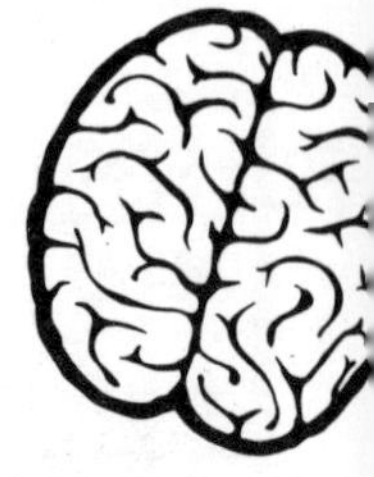

	+	58	=	108
+		-		+
	-	32	=	10
=		=		=
	+	26	=	

PUZZLE 2

44	-		=	6
+		-		+
	+	35	=	53
=		=		=
	-	3	=	

BEAT THE CUBE

Can you fill in each grid with the **letters C, U, B** and **E** once in every row, column and 2x2 box? Too easy? Try completing each puzzle in **less than 60 seconds**. Start the clock!

PUZZLE 1:
Easy

	B	C	
C			E
B	E		
		E	B

seconds

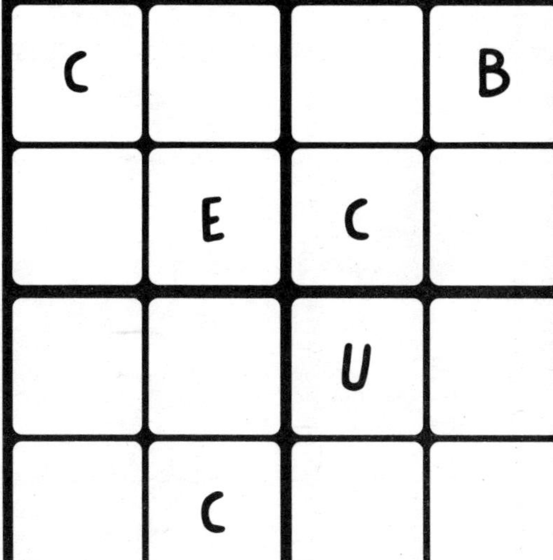

C			B
	E	C	
		U	
	C		

PUZZLE 2:
Medium

seconds

LEVEL 1

WANNA PLAY?

These cubes are all in a scramble! Draw lines to **connect the identical cubes**, then **circle the odd cube out**.

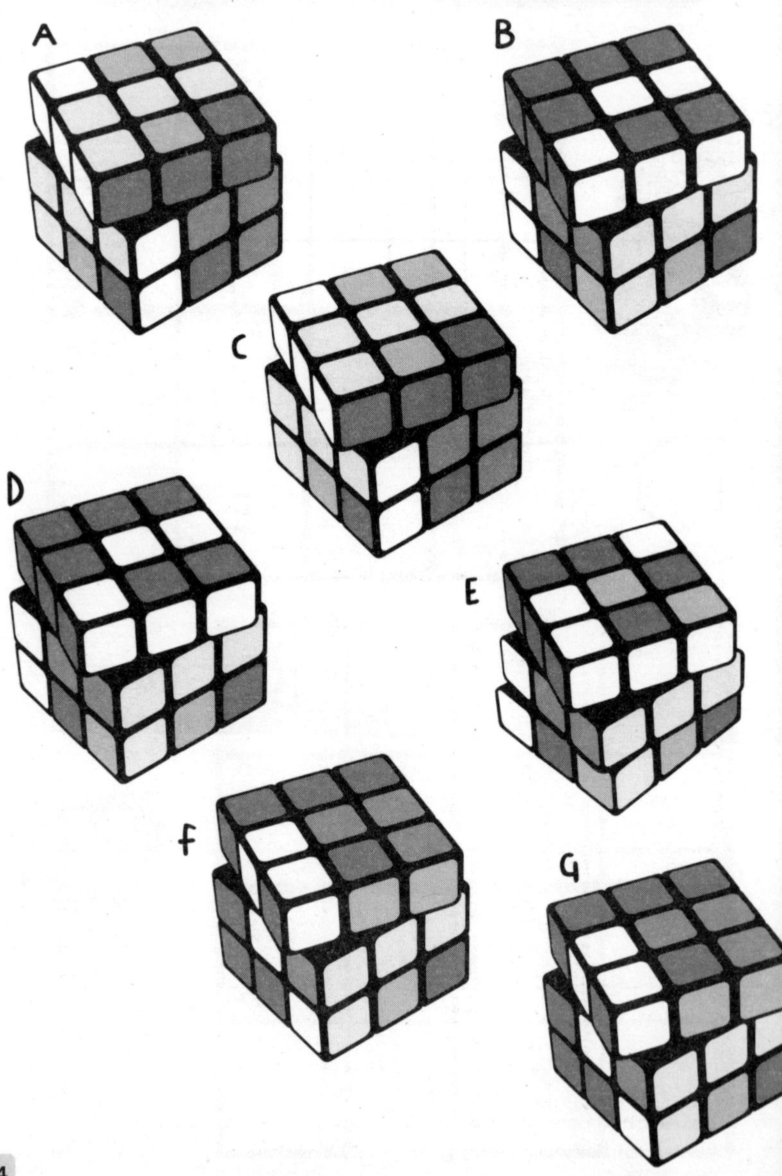

TWENTY IS PLENTY!

Starting at number 1, fill in the missing numbers in order from **1–20**, then **trace a path through the grid**. You can go up, down, forwards or backwards – but **not** diagonally. Watch out for trick numbers!

LEVEL 1

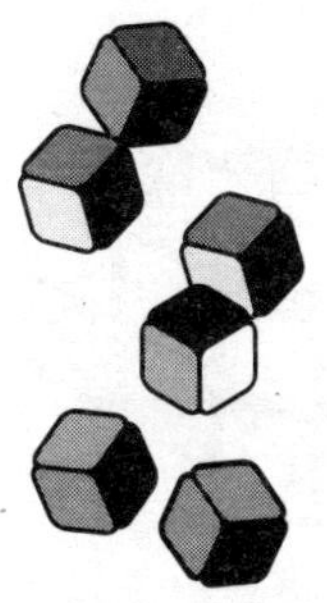

8	7	4	3
9	6	5	2
10	13	14	1
11	12	15	16

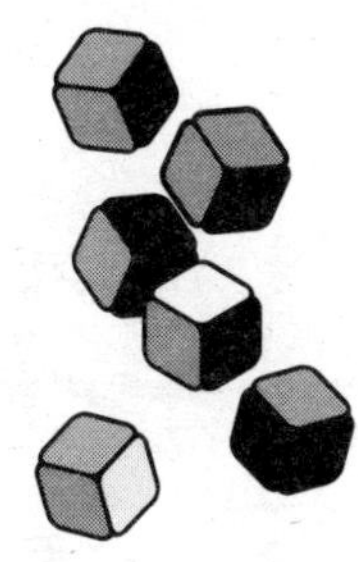

1		3	4	5
	3	18		20
5	6	17		17
6	9		15	14
	8	11		13

LEVEL 1

SEARCH AND SOLVE

Find the following fifteen words familiar to any cube fan in the grid below. The words may appear forwards, backwards, up, down or diagonally.

V	R	H	R	J	O	C	M	Y	W	R	N	N	W	A
E	A	G	S	S	D	U	P	F	F	Q	O	I	Z	T
C	R	E	H	O	D	B	X	R	P	G	D	R	T	E
M	E	N	S	C	L	N	A	J	O	D	W	F	S	A
T	B	I	C	O	D	V	G	H	L	B	R	Z	I	S
H	U	U	R	J	J	O	E	O	P	F	L	M	W	E
I	C	S	A	W	L	B	N	Y	M	P	K	E	T	R
N	B	X	M	R	Y	I	J	A	T	L	O	G	M	S
K	Y	V	B	X	U	W	Y	B	Y	A	Z	B	Z	N
Z	Q	X	L	G	M	B	F	M	B	Y	E	O	R	R
P	A	P	E	A	L	B	I	G	N	E	P	W	P	U
J	P	U	Z	Z	L	E	B	K	A	R	D	N	R	T
V	S	W	S	P	E	E	D	O	S	M	V	B	D	A
M	P	O	H	F	M	T	Z	F	I	J	E	Q	Z	K
B	R	A	I	N	F	V	S	A	G	J	Z	R	T	W

RUBIK'S REBEL

One of these cube faces is not like the others – can you spot which it is? **Circle the rebel pattern.**

LEVEL 1

DON'T MESS UP!

Can you make these squares feel whole again? Connect the shapes in the **left column** with their **missing mini squares**.

1 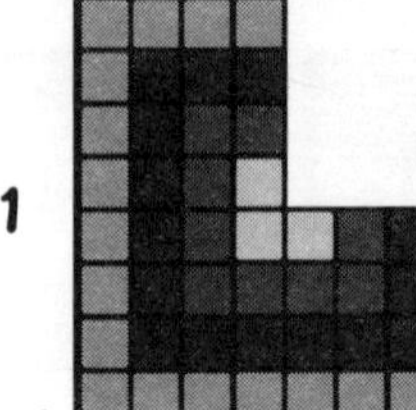

A 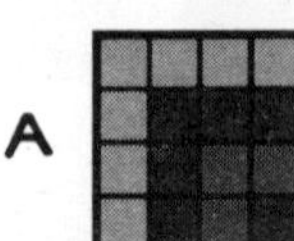

2 

B 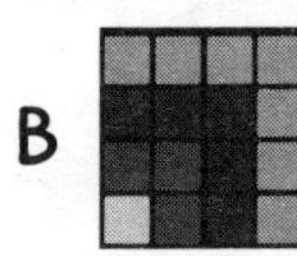

3 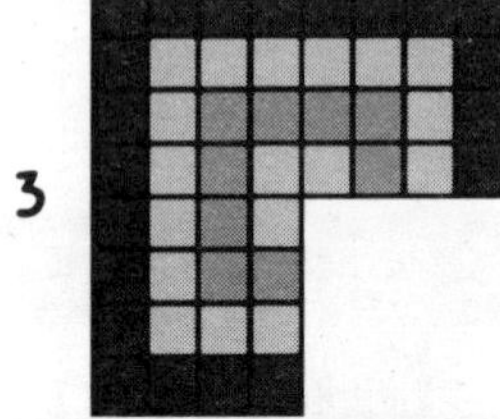

C 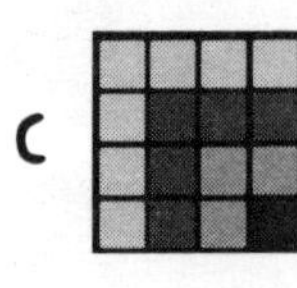

4 

D 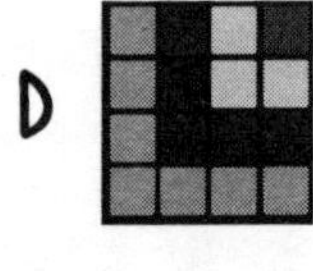

5 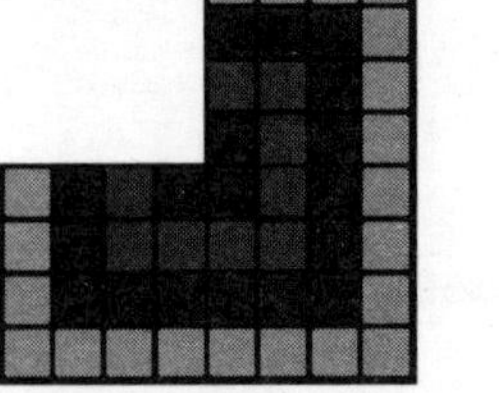

E 

BRAINBUSTER

Here's a puzzle that requires all your grey matter . . . Make your way through the **brain-shaped maze** choosing the quickest route to the finish.

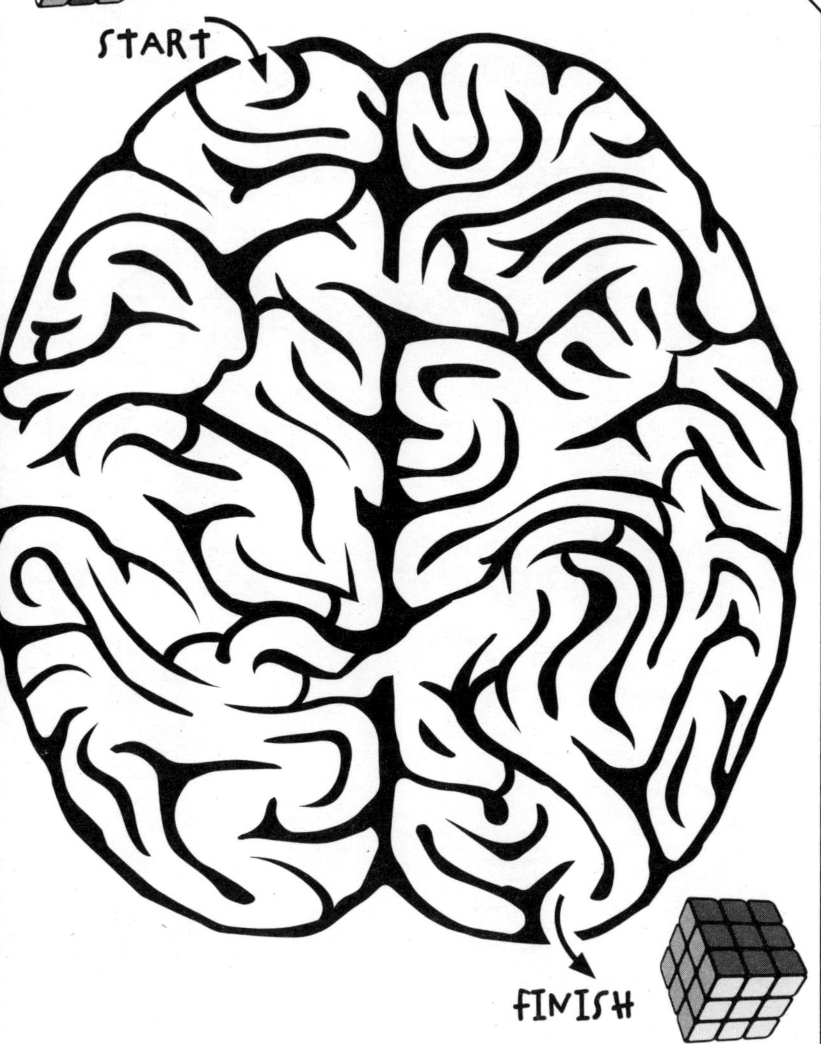

LEVEL 1

WORK OUT

Can you decide **which cube or cubes is missing** from these short sequences? Speed solvers welcome!

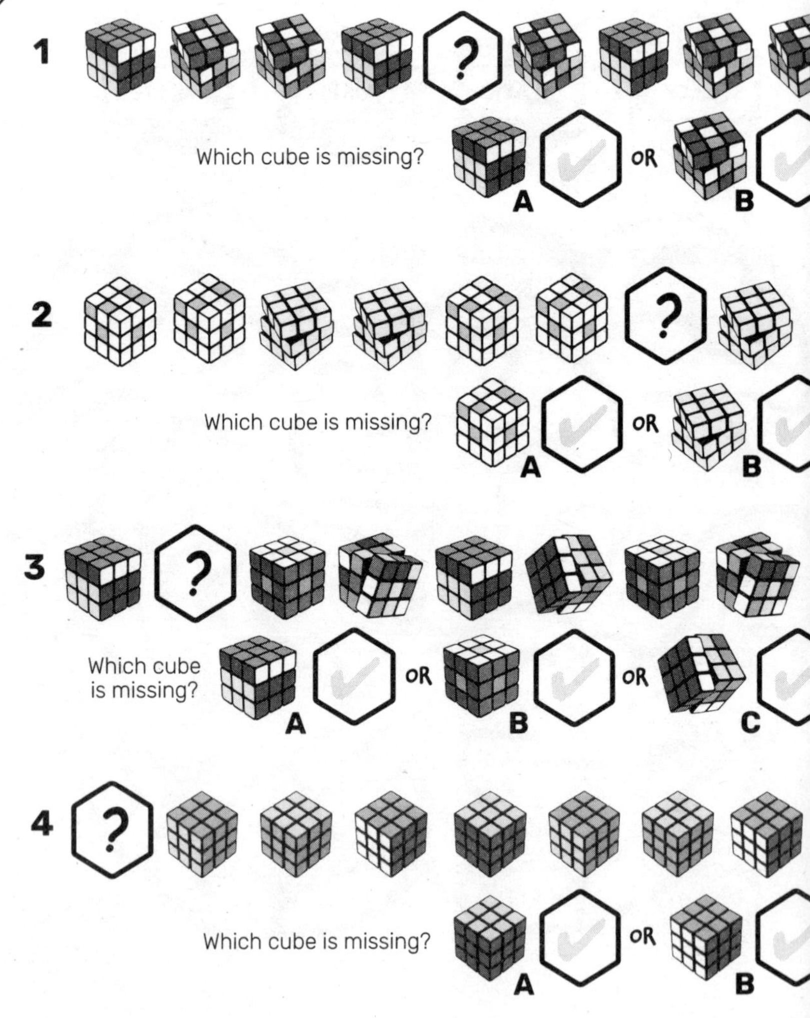

#SPEEDSOLVING

Trace a path **in any direction** from START to FINISH. You must land on **all six cubies** that are **real colours** on a Rubik's Cube.

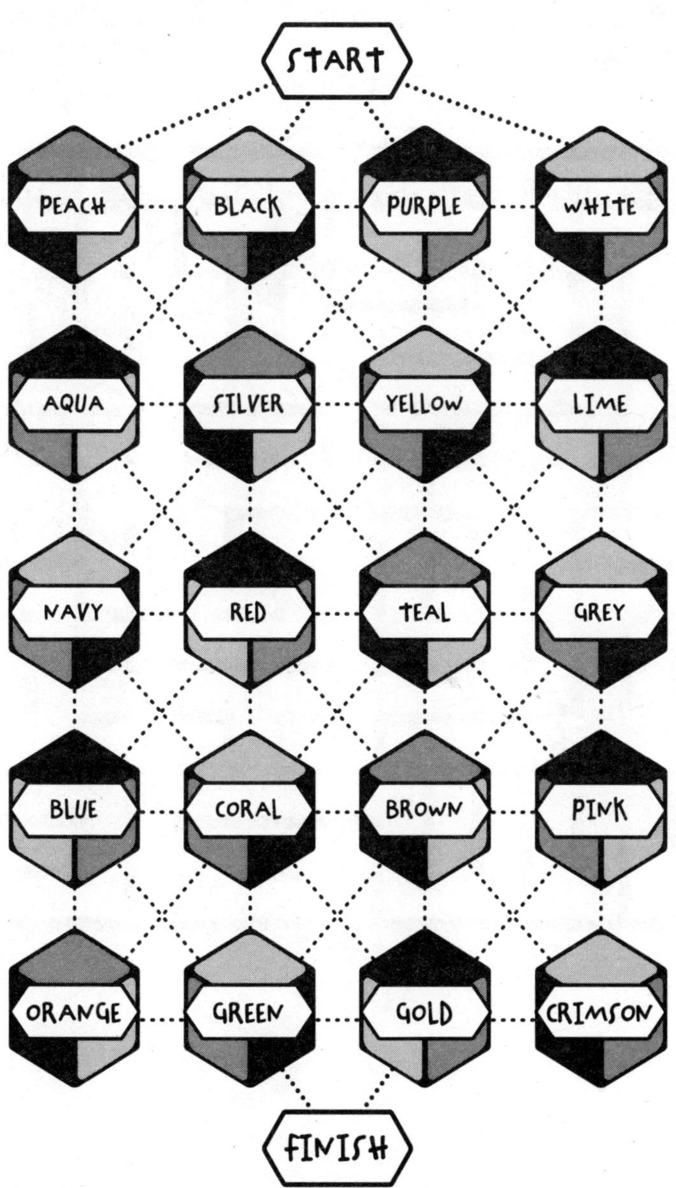

LEVEL 1

LEVEL 1

TWISTS AND TURNS

Find your way to the finish collecting **ten letters** as you go. Now write the letters in **reverse order** to reveal the name of the **original and best puzzle.**

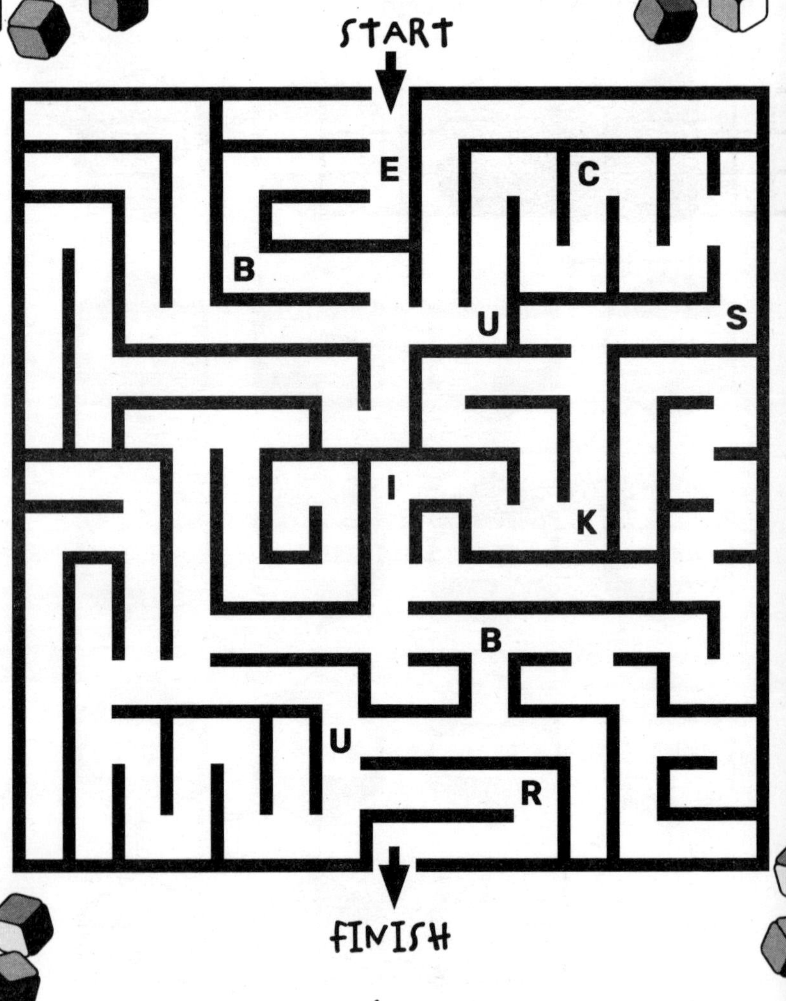

_ _ _ _ _ _   _ _ _ _

PROBLEM SOLVED

This puzzle might just blow your mind! **Tick the flat net that exactly matches this cube.**

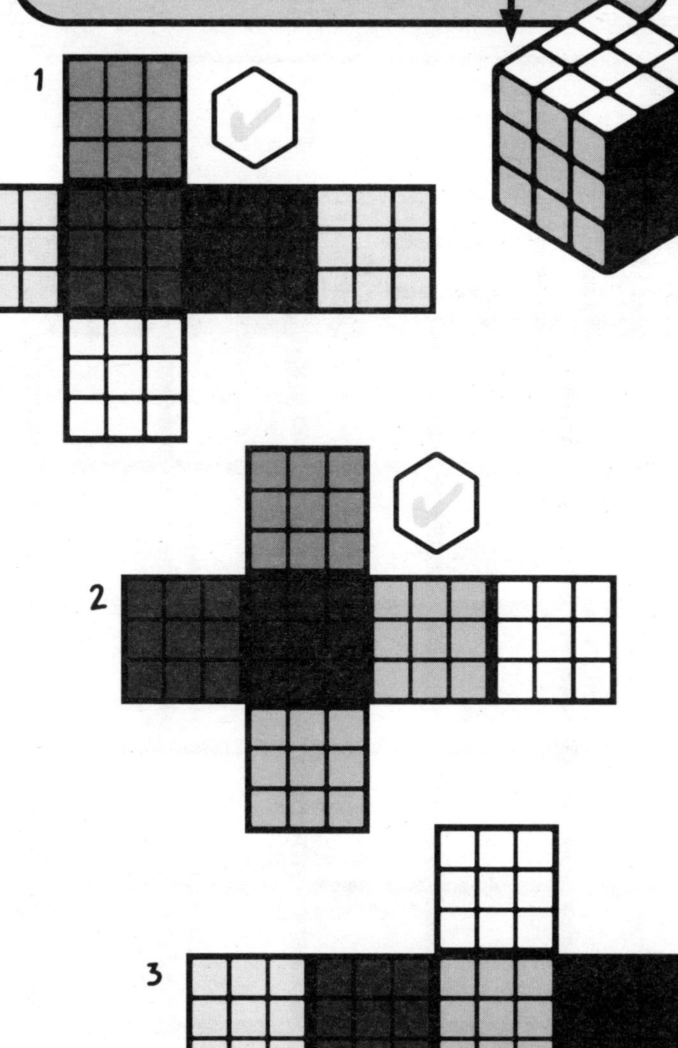

TIC-TAC-GO!

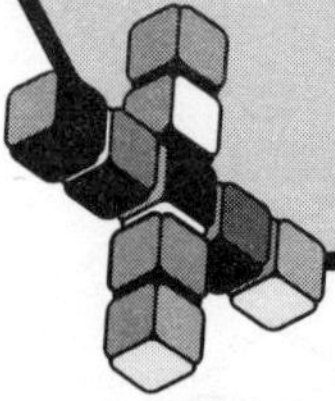

Challenge another cuber to see who comes out on top in this **mega game of tic-tac-toe**. Grab a pen each and tic-tac-GO!

RULES:

- One player plays as **X** and the other as **O.**
- Take turns to make your mark in the empty cubies.
- If a player completes a row of **three Xs or Os** (up, down, across or diagonally), they **score a point.**
- The winner is the player with the most points once **every cubie** on the grid has been filled.

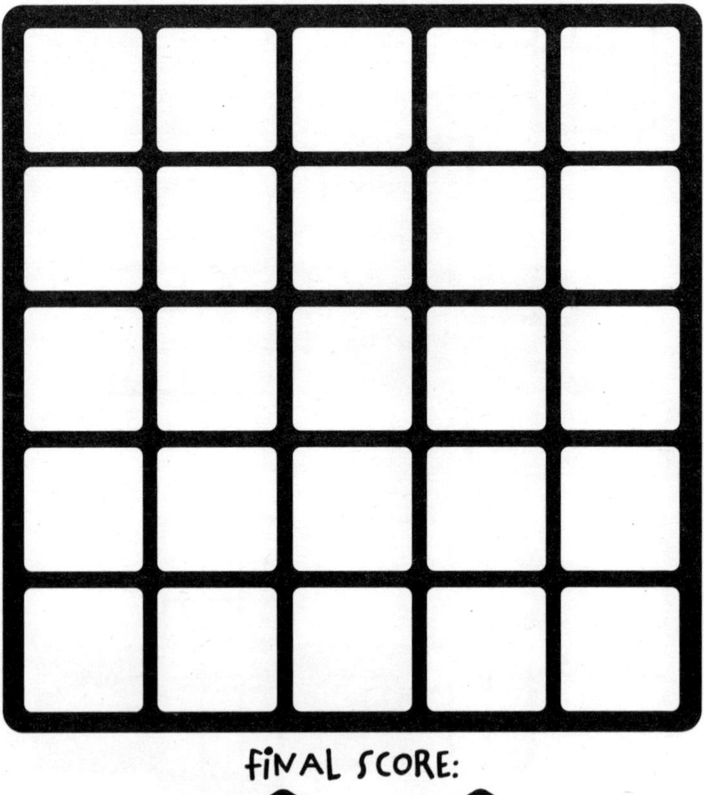

FINAL SCORE:

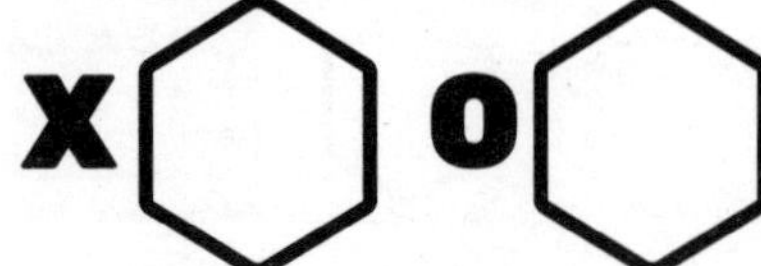

FUTOSHIKI FUN

Place the **numbers 1 to 4** so that they appear **once only** in each row and column. Pay attention to the **greater than (>)** and **less than (<) symbols** between some of the cubies – these helpful hints can help you complete the grids faster!

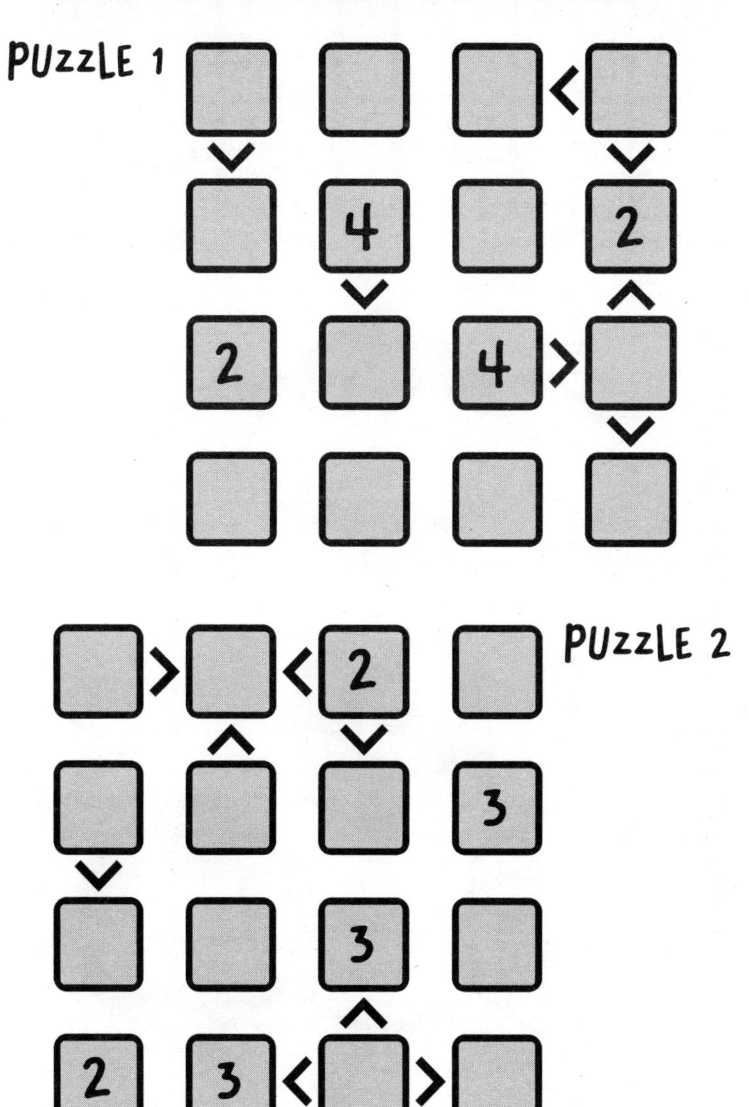

LEVEL 1

LEVEL 1

CODEBREAKER

Complete the key, then **decode the words on each cube** to reveal the cuber's way of life!

A	B	C	D	E	F	G	H	I	J	K	L	M
	25	24						18				
N	**O**	**P**	**Q**	**R**	**S**	**T**	**U**	**V**	**W**	**X**	**Y**	**Z**
13				9								1

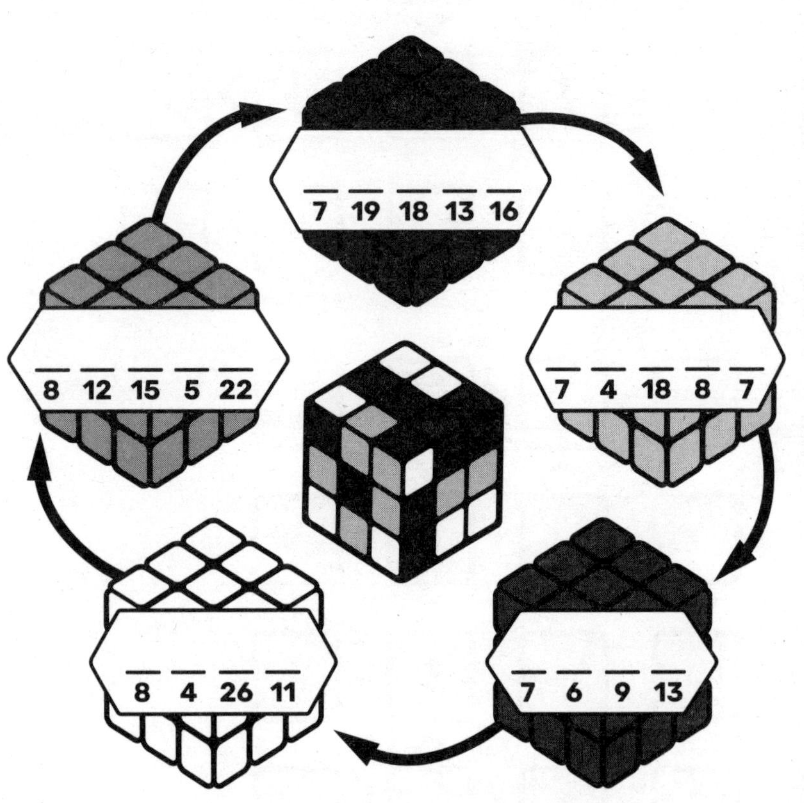

CUBE CONNECTION

Check out the cool cube below! Without counting, **estimate the number of cubies** that make up each path from end to end. Then **count the cubies** to see if you were right. Beware: the same cubie may appear on two faces of the cube.

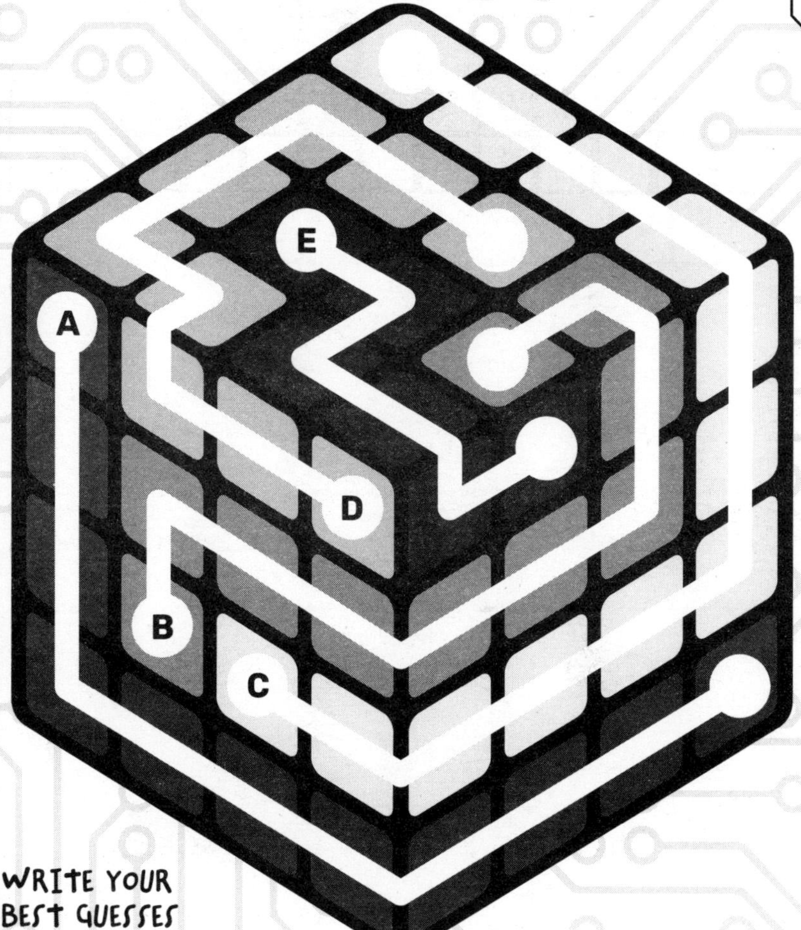

LEVEL 1

A B C D E

WRITE YOUR BEST GUESSES HERE:

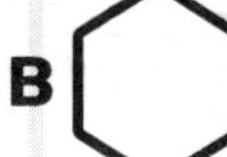

LEVEL 2

CUBIE KINGS AND QUEENS

Take on another keen cuber in this **royally good game!**

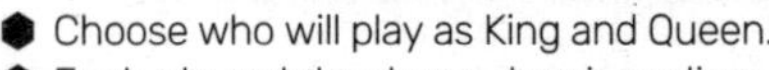

- Choose who will play as King and Queen.
- Each player takes turns drawing a line (no diagonal lines) to join two dots.
- If the line completes a 1x1 square, the player marks either **K** or **Q** inside, and draws another line.
- The game is over when lines have been joined to all the dots on the grid.
- The player with the most filled 1x1 squares wins!
- A square each has been completed to get you started.

K Q

FINAL SCORE:

KING:	QUEEN:

LEVEL 2

RUBIK'S REVEAL

Grab your pens and pencils and **get colouring!** Use the same **light pencil or pen** to shade the first list of squares, then use a **darker shade** for the second list of squares. Prepare to be amazed!

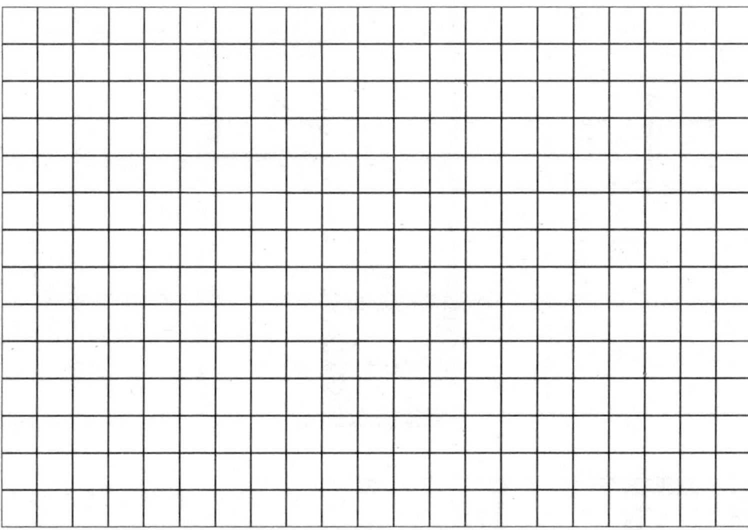

LIGHT SQUARES:

B9–B13, C9, C13,
D9, D11, D13,
E9–E11, E13,
G9–G13, H9, H11, H13,
I9, I11, I13,
J9, J13, L9–L13,
M9, M11, M13,
N9, N11, N13, O9, O13
Q9–Q13, R11, S10, S12,
T9, T13

DARK SQUARES:

A1–A7, B1, B7,
C1, C3–C5, C7, D1, D3–5, D7,
E1, E3–E5, E7, F1–F7, G1, G7,
H1–H3, H5–H7, I1–I3, I5–I7,
J1–J3, J5–J7,
K1, K7, L1–L7
M1, M7, N1–N7, O1, O7
P1, P3–P5, P7, Q1, Q3–Q5, Q7
R1, R3–R5, R7, S1–S7,
T1, T3, T7, U1–U7

LEVEL 2

SHADING IT

Coloured pens or pencils at the ready! Can you fill in **every row, column** and **mini grid** using the **four different colours** below **once each**?

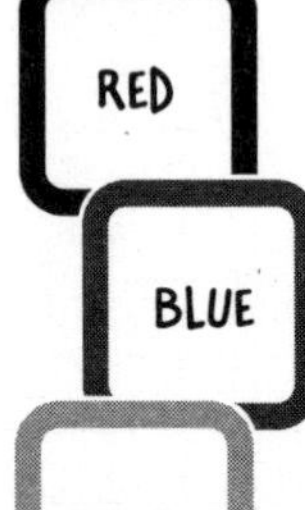

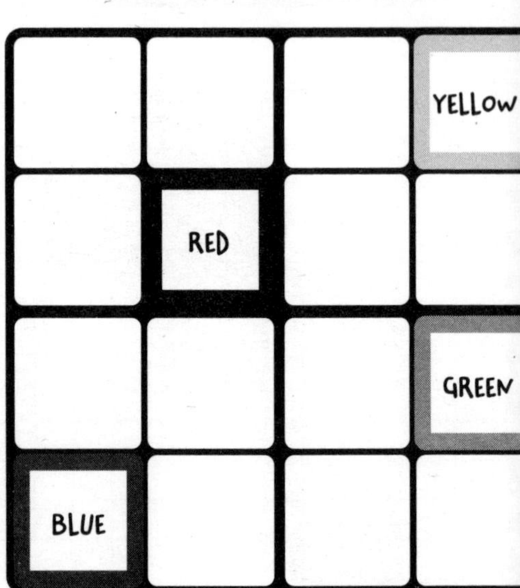

BLUE			
		YELLOW	
RED			
			GREEN

PUZZLE 2

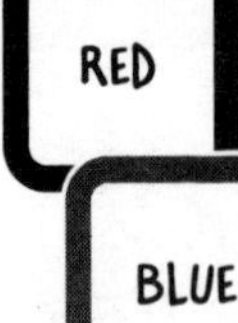

GREEN

YELLOW

VIEW FROM THE TOP

This next puzzle could prove a stumbling block! Take a look at the 3D blocks picture, then decide which option is the **correct view from above**. It's trickier than you might think.

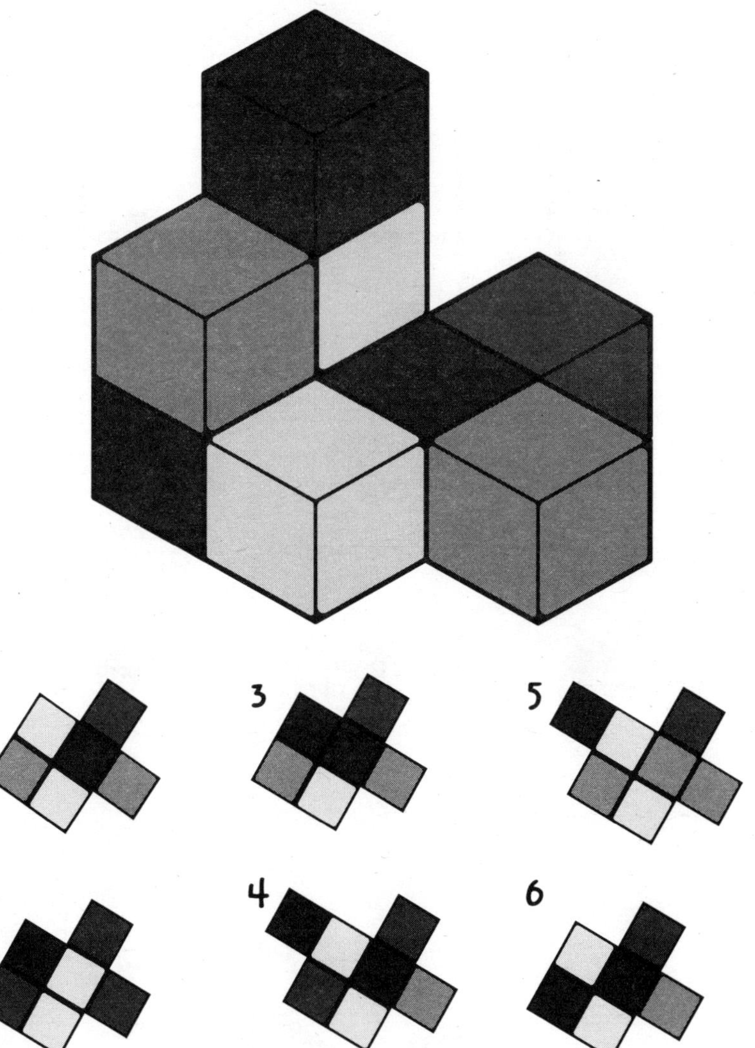

LEVEL 2

NINE INTO FOUR?

Here's a headscratcher for you. Without lifting your pen or pencil from the paper, **draw four straight lines that touch all nine cubes below.** Tip: think outside the box!

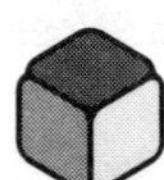  

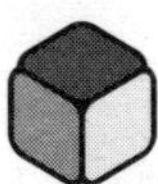 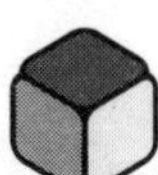 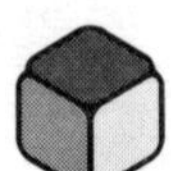

HIDDEN MESSAGE

A **secret message** is contained in this cube face. Can you work out what it says? If you get stuck, try **reversing the problem!**

LEVEL 2

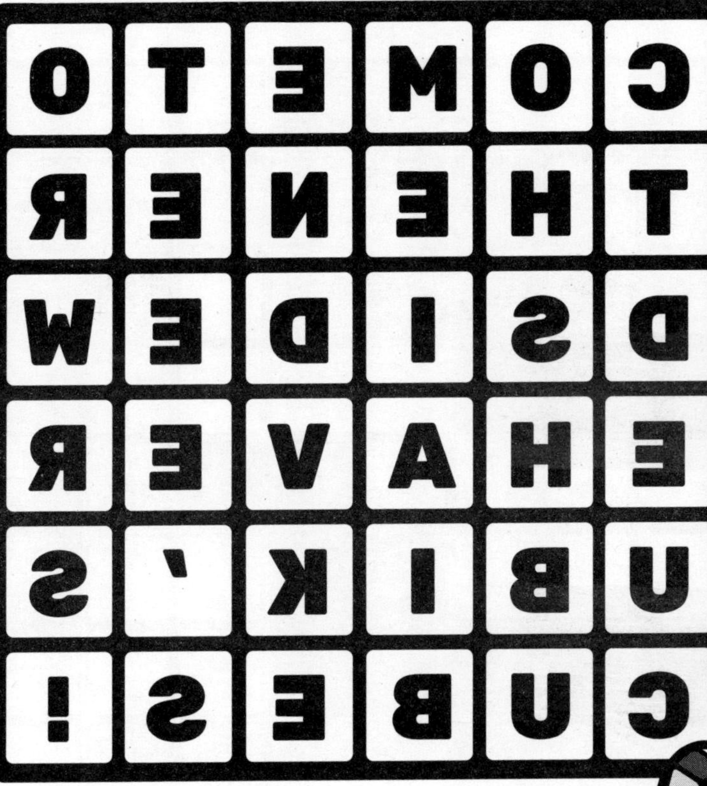

LEVEL 2

OFF GRID

Ready to power up your puzzle skills? Count **how many of each different shape** appear in the grid. The shapes may be rotated, but **not flipped.** Which shape is not in the grid? Put an **X** in the box.

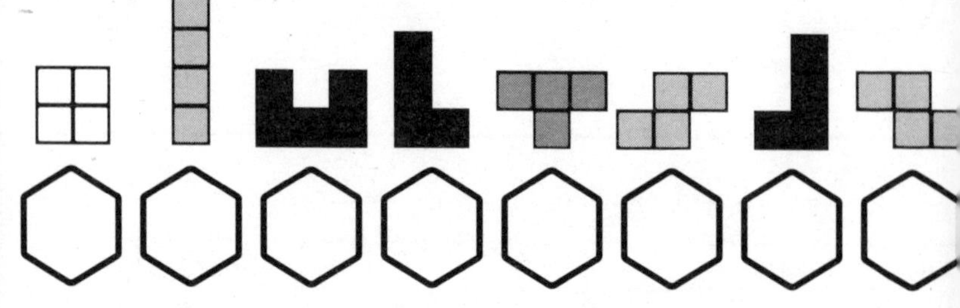

SOLVE IT!

How quickly can you solve this next Cube-inspired puzzle? Place all of the words in the grid **once**, so that they read either **across or down** with one letter per box. Tip: try starting with the **longer words.**

LEVEL

2

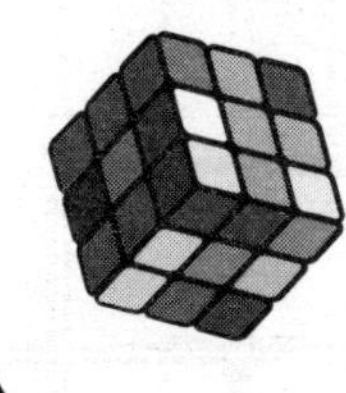

4-letter word
CUBE

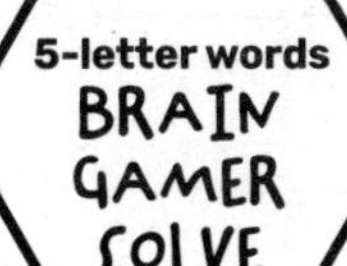

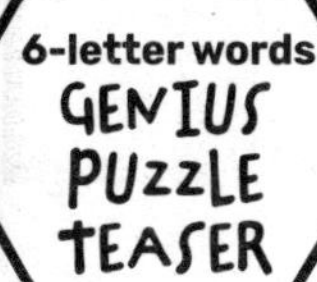

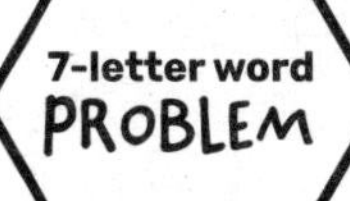

LEVEL 2

RUBIK'S RIDDLE

Use your smarts to work out the **six clues** below correctly and reveal a **hidden word.**

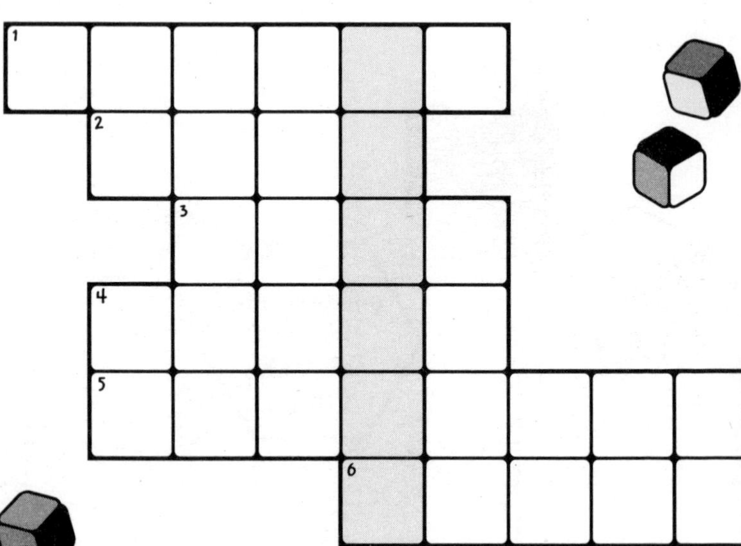

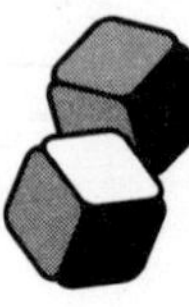

1. A colour on the Cube that's also a fruit.
2. The shape of the classic puzzle created by Ernõ Rubik.
3. This puzzle might just blow your ____!
4. The organ you'll need most to solve a Rubik's Cube.
5. The answer to a problem is known as a ________.
6. Something you'll need to complete a Cube FAST!

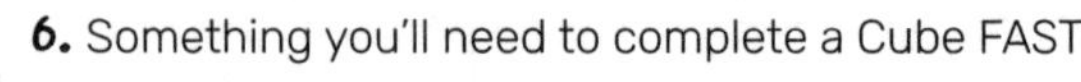

THE HIDDEN WORD IS:

____ ____ ____ ____ ____ ____

AERIAL ACTION

To solve this next puzzle, try approaching the problem from a **different angle!** Study the 3D blocks picture, then choose the **correct aerial view.**

LEVEL 2

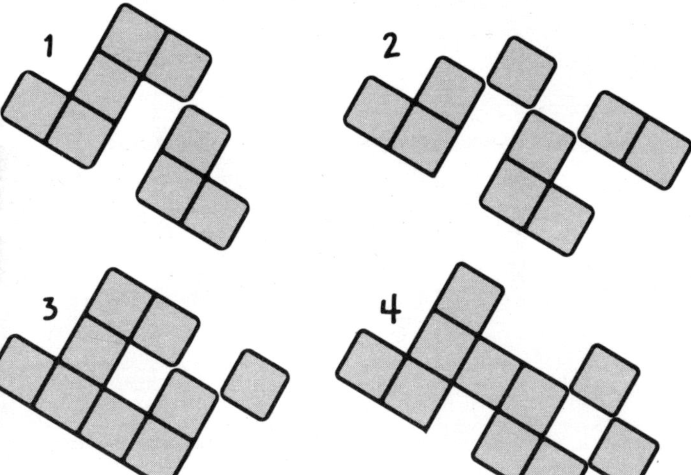

LEVEL 2

PYRAMID PUZZLER

Let's shake things up with a new shape – **the pyramid!** Complete the puzzle by writing a number in every empty cubie. Numbers that appear in cubies **next to each other** must **add up** to the number in the one **directly above.**

Tip: Start at the bottom and things will soon add up!

Example:

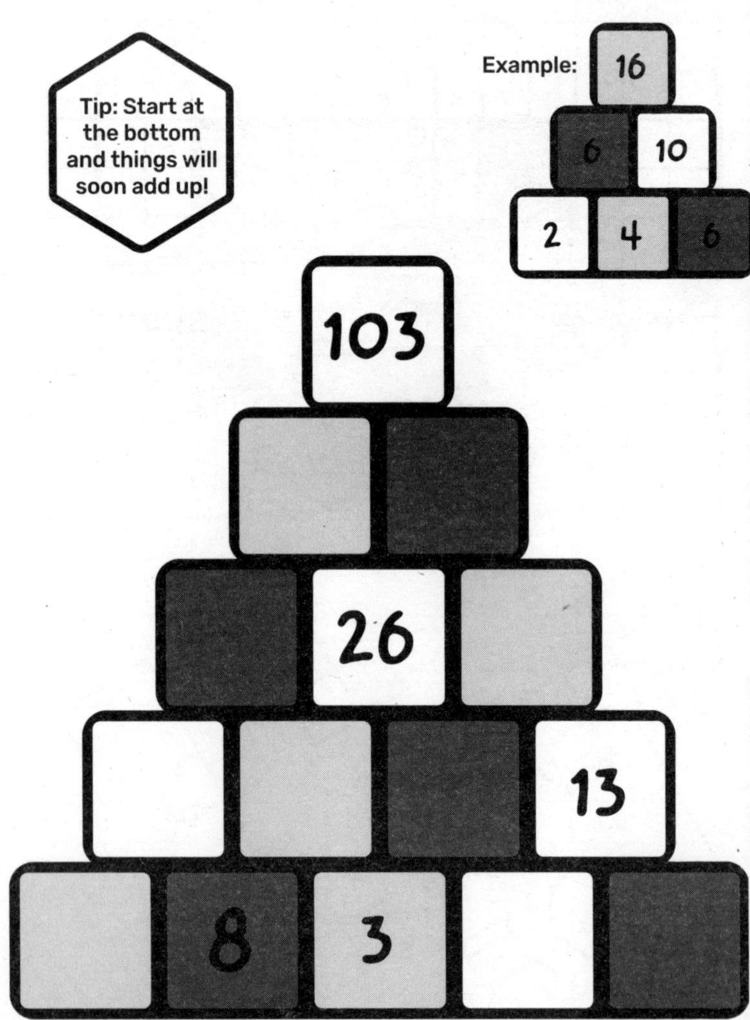

TOTALLY TOUGH

Take aim, hotshot puzzlers! For each sum, choose **one number in the outer ring**, **one** in the next **inner ring** and **one in the centre ring** to make the **total scores** below. Numbers can be used again.

LEVEL 2

14
7
8
13
11
6
3
9
10
12
5
4

TOTAL SCORES TO MAKE:

☐ + ☐ + ☐ = 16

☐ + ☐ + ☐ = 32

☐ + ☐ + ☐ = 37

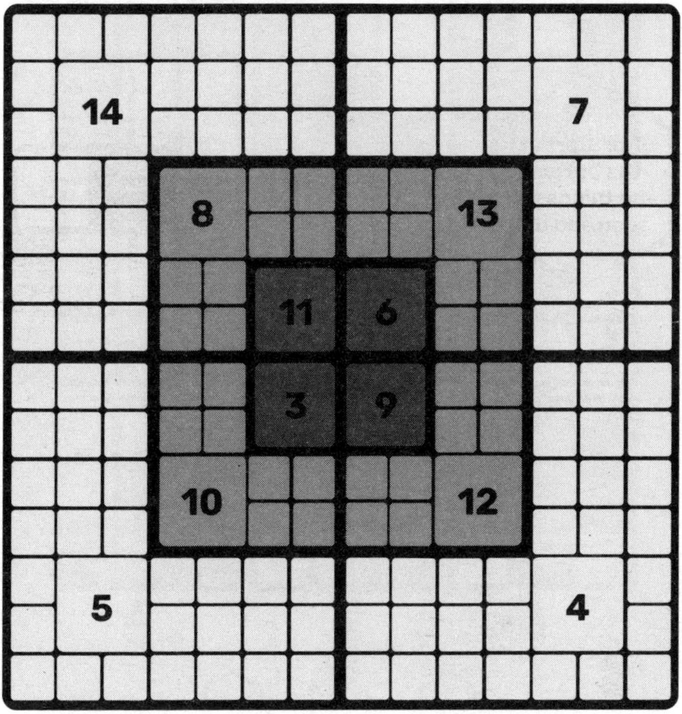

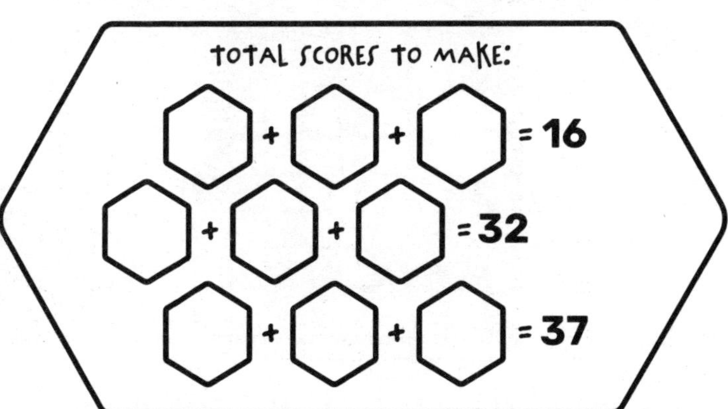

LEVEL 2

LOVE TO PLAY

How much do you ♥ the Cube? Put the picture in the correct order shown below, writing numbers in the boxes. **No flipping allowed!**

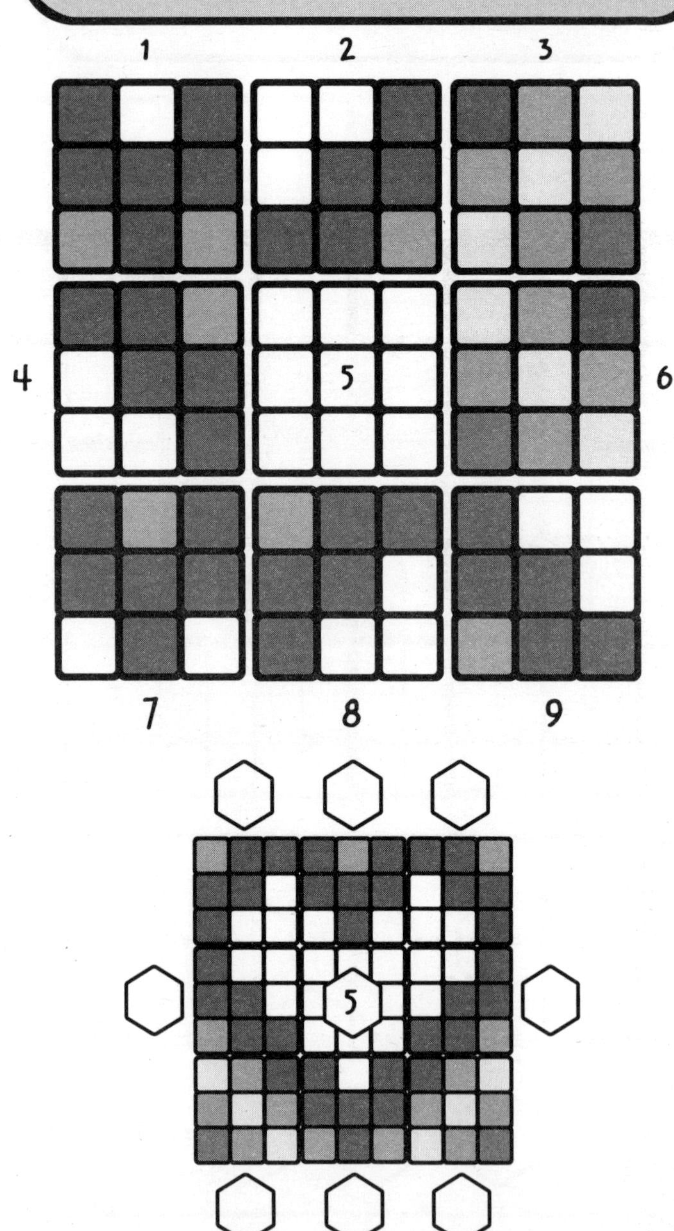

FIVE LIVES

Shade in five more squares to make your way through the **blocky maze** to the finish. You can move up, down, left or right on the shaded squares only. Diagonal moves are not allowed.

LEVEL 2

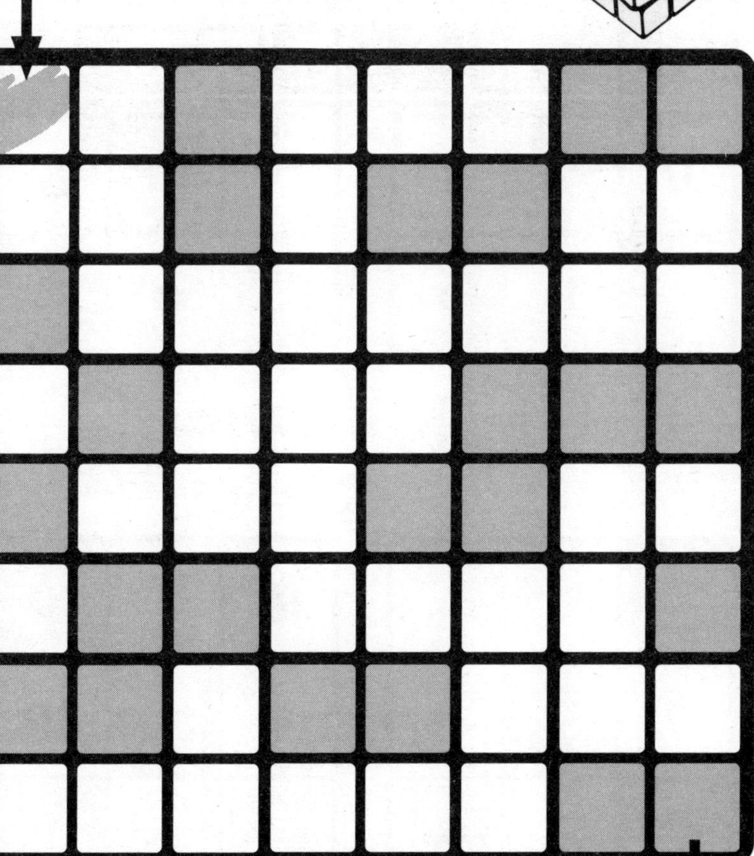

MAGIC SQUARES

Solve these puzzles before your eyes turn square! Complete the squares so that the **numbers add up to the same number in each column, row and diagonal line**. The **same number cannot appear twice** in each grid.

	3	10
9		5
	11	6

1. total =

7		
	10	8
	6	13

2. total =

5	9	
	7	8

3. total = 27

18		10
4		20

4. total =

ALL SQUARE

Just squares, don't care! Look closely at the picture – **how many squares can you count altogether?**

LEVEL 2

MY ANSWER =

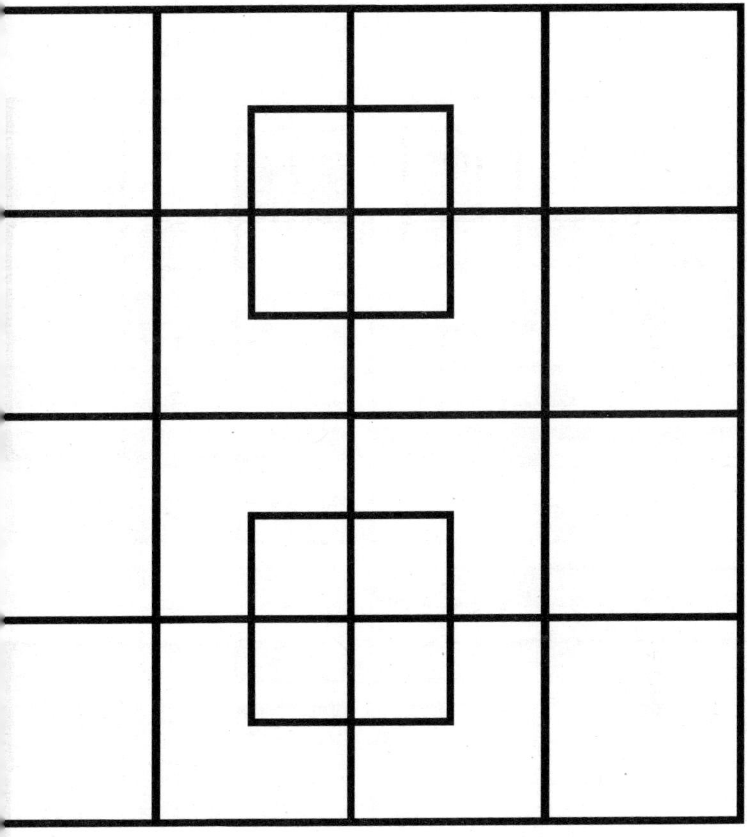

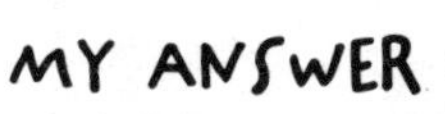

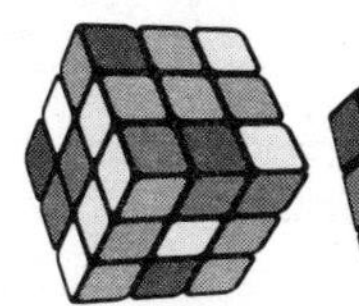

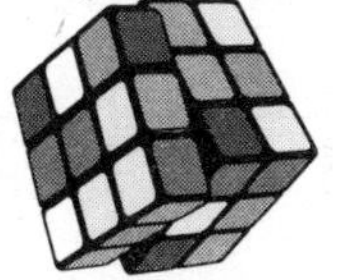

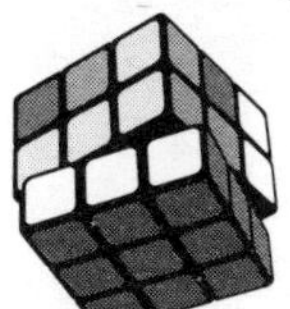

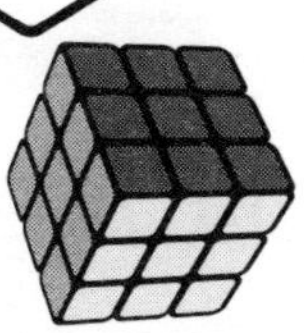

LEVEL 2

UNIQUE CUBE

Only those with the sharpest spotting skills will pass this next test! Circle the **only cube face** on the page that is **different from the rest.**

SQUARE EYES

All set for your eye test? Let's go! See how quickly can you find the **mini squares** in the **bigger grid.** Remember, the mini ones must **match exactly.**

LEVEL 2

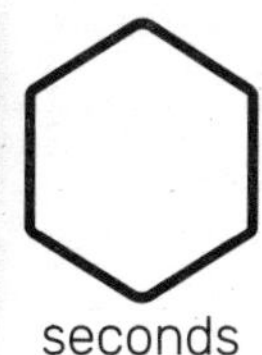

seconds

2

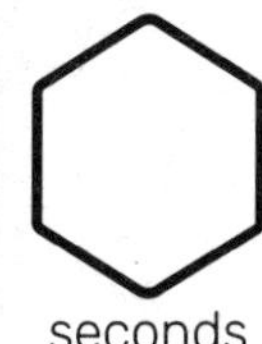

seconds

LEVEL 2

GRUDGE MATCH

Ready for a **rematch**? Or will you challenge a new opponent? Either way, a contest fit for a **king** and a **queen** awaits!

- Choose who will play as King and Queen.
- Each player takes turns drawing a line (no diagonal lines) to join two dots.
- If the line completes a 1x1 square, the player marks either **K** or **Q** inside, and draws another line.
- The game is over when lines have been joined to all the dots on the g
- The player with the most filled 1x1 squares wins!
- A square each has been complete to get you started.

K Q

FiNAL SCORE:

KING:	QUEEN:

TOUGH TEST

Add the **missing numbers** to these grids so that everything **multiplies** and **divides** perfectly. Live it, breathe it, solve it!

LEVEL 2

PUZZLE 1

40	÷		=	2
x		÷		x
3	x		=	
=		=		=
120	÷		=	60

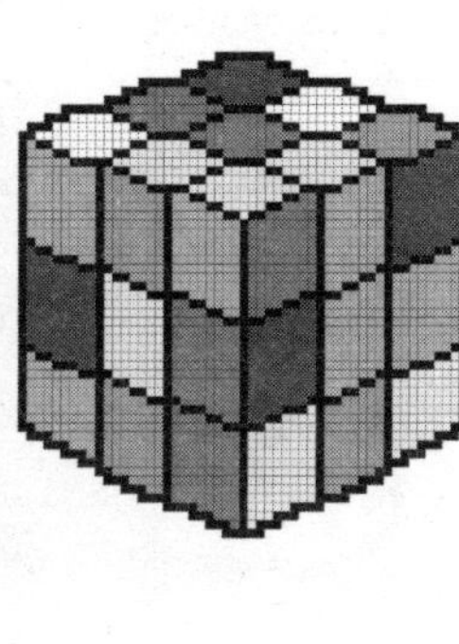

PUZZLE 2

10	÷		=	2
x		x		x
24	÷	8	=	
=		=		=
	÷		=	6

LEVEL 2

PUZZLE PATH

Elite cubers always find a way! Can you follow the path in number order from **1 to 25**? Choose carefully – one wrong turn and it's game over! Move **up, down, left or right,** one cubie at a time.

1	2	3	5	19	21
2	8	6	7	10	20
3	4	5	8	23	24
12	11	10	9	22	23
13	16	17	18	21	24
14	15	20	19	20	25

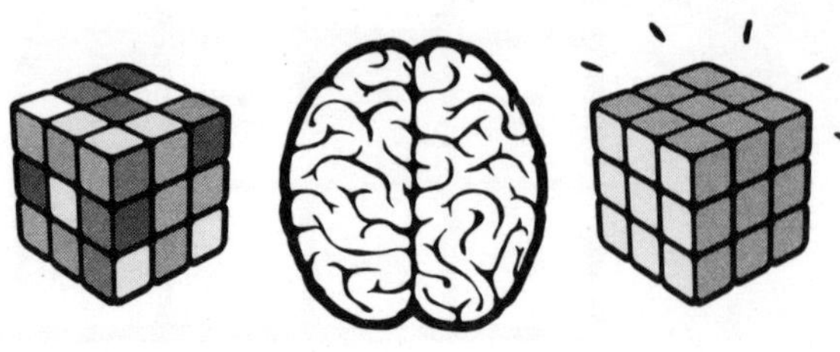

NEXT LEVEL

More Futoshiki fun, only this time there are **five fiendish numbers** to add to the grid. Place the numbers 1 to 5 so that they appear **once only** in each row and column. Don't forget to follow the **greater than (>)** and **less than (<) symbols.**

LEVEL 2

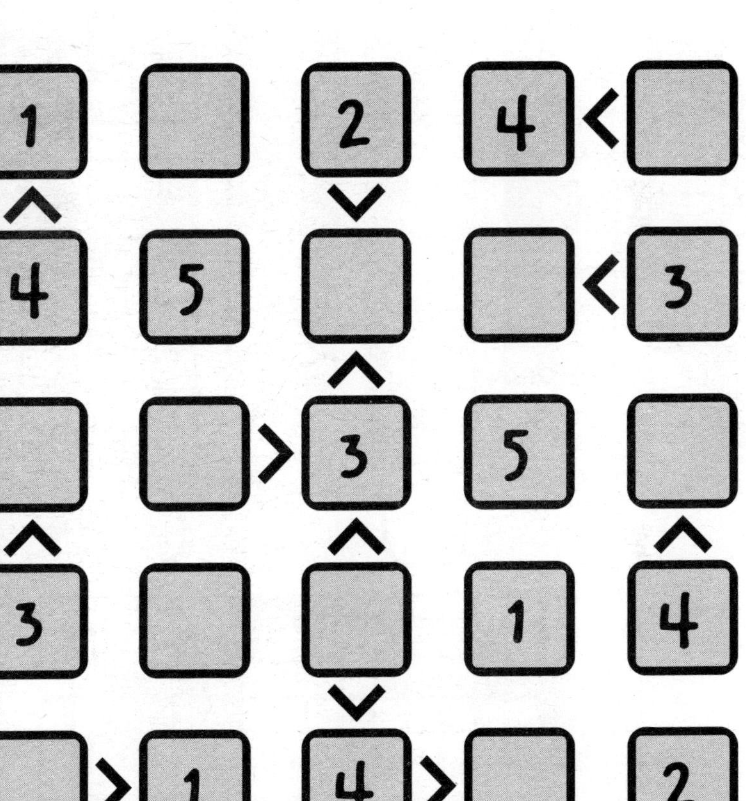

LEVEL 2

RUBIK'S RAINBOW

Can you put the columns back in the right order to reveal **Rubik's Rainbow**? Check out the completed rainbow below as a guide.

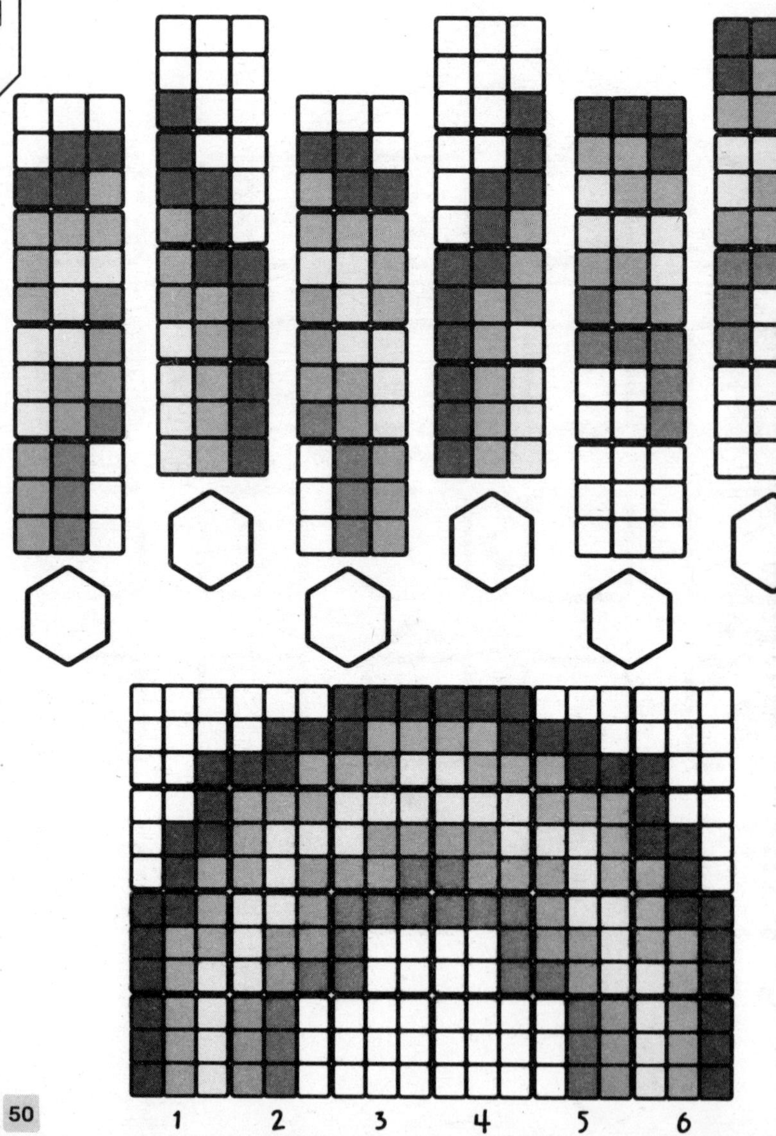

MASTER CUBE

Have you got the smarts to beat this next-level cube? **Estimate the number of cubies** that make up each path, then **count them**. The same cubie may appear on more than one cube face.

LEVEL 2

RITE YOUR
ST GUESSES
RE:

A B C D

E F G H

LEVEL 2

DARE TO PAIR

Get counting, then draw lines to **connect pairs** of shifting shapes that share the **same number of cubies.** Totally tricky!

1

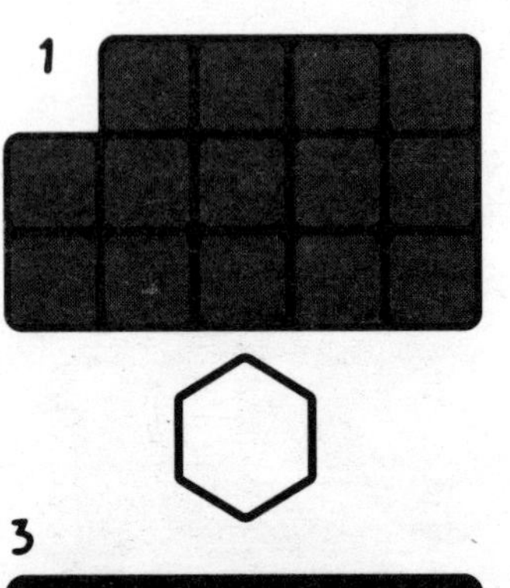

2

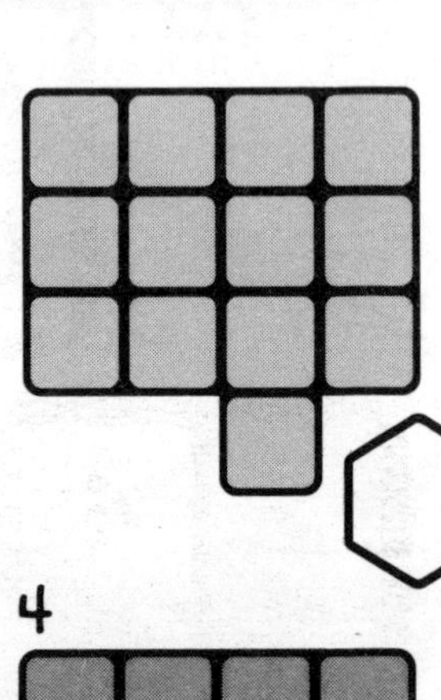

3

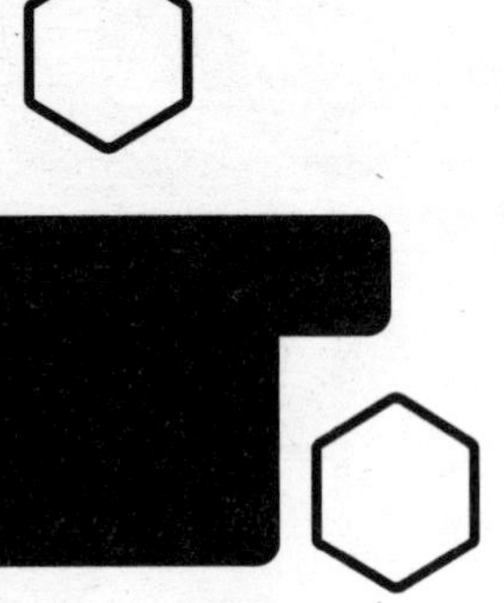

4

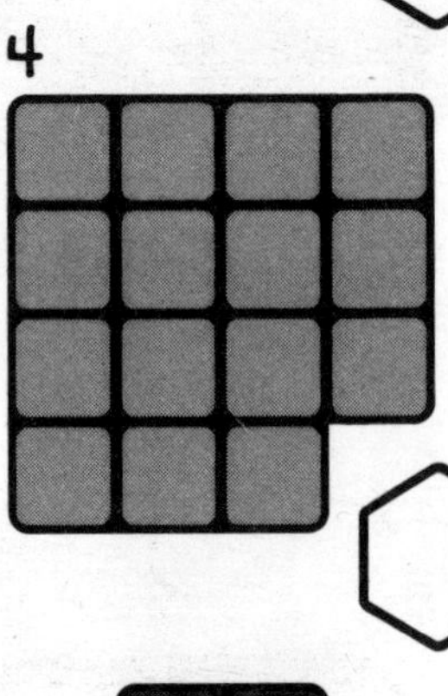

5

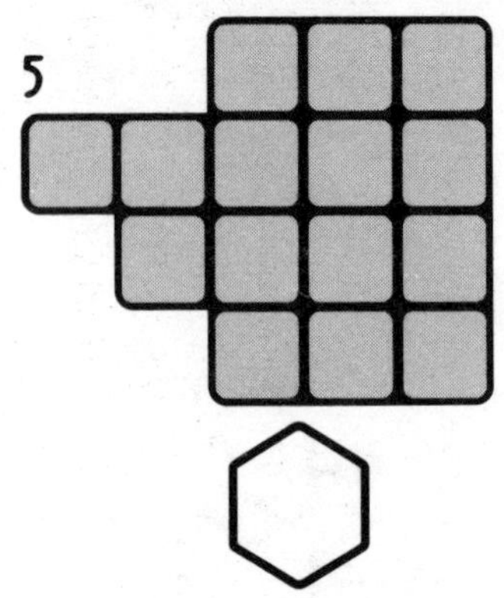

6

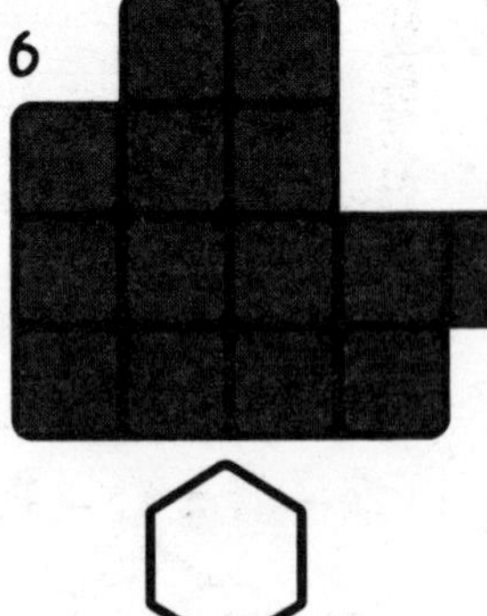

M.I.A.

Cubers look for solutions not problems! Study the **formula,** then work out the **missing number** in each number grid.

LEVEL 3

KEY:

A	B
C	D

1

A + D = B + C

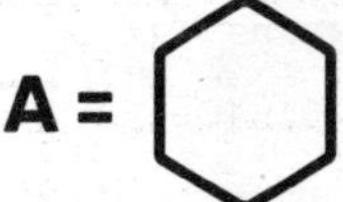

2

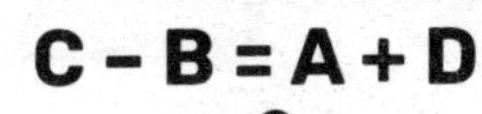

B =

3

A – D = C – B

C =

4

3	7
6	?

A + B = C + D

D =

LEVEL 3

SHAPING UP

Here's hoping these puzzles shape up nicely for you! Place the **numbers 1 to 5 once only** in each column, row and mini shape.

PUZZLE 1

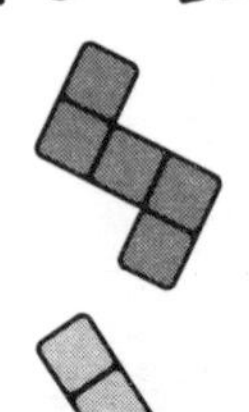

5	1			
4			2	3
	4			
	2			5

PUZZLE 2

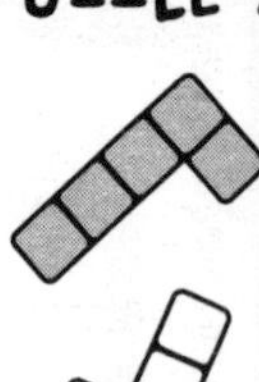

5	1			
	2		4	
			1	
	3			1
4				3

GAMER TAG

OK, cubers, it's time to level up. Write the letters of the word **GAMER** once each in every row and column of the grid, and so that two identical letters **never touch** – not even diagonally.

LEVEL 3

	M		R	
E				M
M				A
	G		M	

CUBE NUMBERS

When you multiply a number by itself, then multiply it again, you get a **cube number.** Clever, eh! **Write the sum, draw the missing cubes or both** to show each cube number.

A 1 x 1 x 1 = 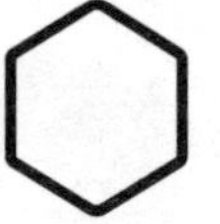 

B 2 x 2 x 2 =

C 3 x 3 x 3 =

D 4 x 4 x 4 =

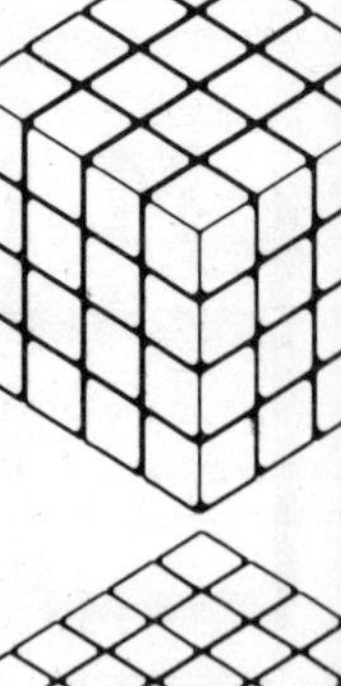

E 5 x 5 x 5 = 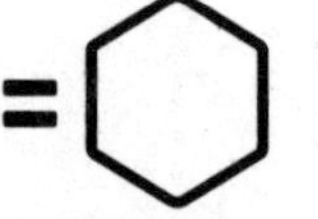

FACE VALUE

Each of the three shaded cubies below has a **different value, less than ten.** One has been solved for you. Give your brain a workout and **find the value of the other two cubie shades.**

=

= 3

=

LEVEL 3

NO SCORE FOUR

Another game for two players to tackle, but as with the famous cube, this one comes with a twist! Fill the grid with **Xs and 0s,** scoring by drawing **three in a row.** Draw four though, and you'll **lose a point!**

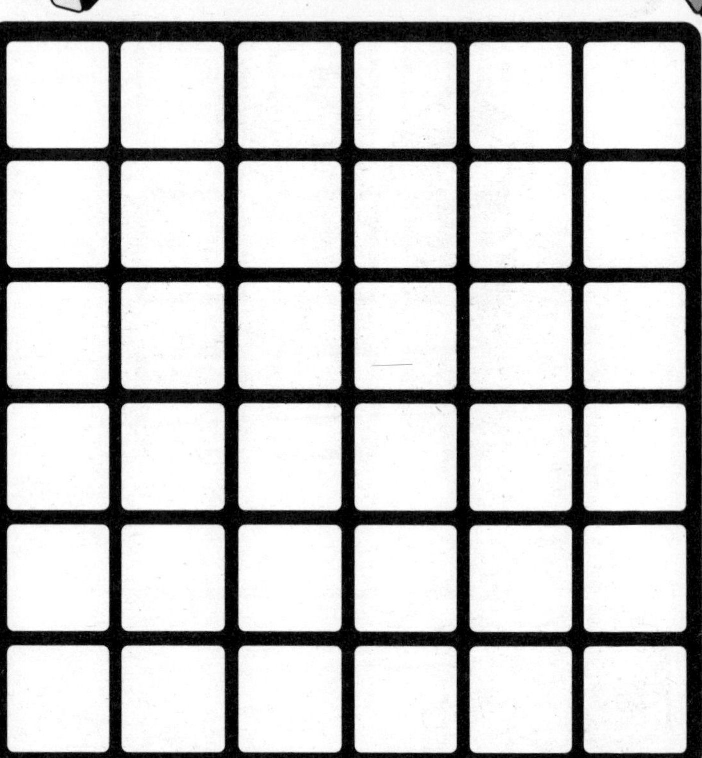

HOW TO PLAY:

- Decide who will play as **X** and **0**, then take turns placing an **X or 0** in the grid, until there are no empty cubies.
- Score a point by completing **three Xs or 0s in a row** (vertically, horizontally or diagonally).
- **Deduct a point** if a row of **four Xs or 0s** is drawn!

FINAL SCORE:

PLAYER 1	PLAYER 2

A MULTITUDE OF CUBES!

Together, these cubes form quite the collection. How many Rubik's Cubes can you count **altogether**? Tick the box with the **correct number.**

LEVEL 3

22 ☐ **25** ☐ **28** ☐

LEVEL 3

WORD UP

This next puzzle will separate the cubers from the noobs! Fill in the cubies with **words of different lengths** using the letters that make up **RUBIK'S CUBE**.

Note: o
the lette
and **U** ca
used tw

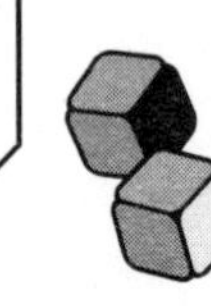

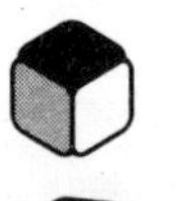

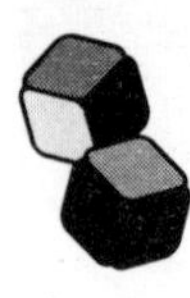

CUBER'S QUIZ

Curious facts or twists on the truth? How much do you know about the fiendishly fun puzzle that is the **Rubik's Cube?** Tick **true or false** after each statement.

LEVEL 3

1 The original cube was designed by Hungarian architect Ernő Rubik. **TRUE** **FALSE**

2 There are more than 43 quintillion possible puzzle combinations when twisting and turning a Rubik's Cube. **TRUE** **FALSE**

3 Nine different colours appear on a Rubik's Cube. **TRUE** **FALSE**

4 No matter how mixed-up, a Rubik's Cube can be solved in twenty moves or fewer. **TRUE** **FALSE**

5 The world record for solving a 3x3x3 Cube in the fastest time is a super-speedy 3.13 seconds. **TRUE** **FALSE**

6 The Rubik's Cube was invented in 1970. **TRUE** **FALSE**

7 The puzzle was originally called the 'Magic Cube' when it was first released. **TRUE** **FALSE**

8 Ernő Rubik may have invented the clever cube puzzle, but even he struggled to solve it the first time! **TRUE** **FALSE**

LEVEL 3

OVERVIEW

More blocks to unlock! Study the bigger picture, then choose the correct **bird's-eye view**. Don't forget any **hidden cubies**.

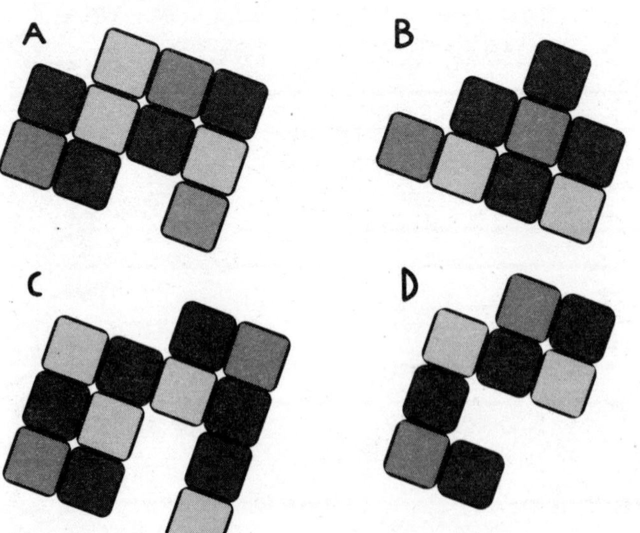

WIN THE SIM!

This next game called Sim will separate the champs from the chumps – decide carefully which puzzle-lover you're ready to challenge! Each grab a **different-coloured pen** before starting.

LEVEL 3

HOW TO PLAY:

- The aim of the game is for players to **avoid completing a triangle in their own colour.**
- Take turns drawing over the grey lines between two dots until all the lines are coloured.
- Complete a triangle in your own colour and it's **game over!**

Warning: the game cannot end in a draw without a triangle being drawn.

MATCH 1:

Warm-Up

Winner:

....

MATCH 2:

Second Chance

Winner:

....

LEVEL 3

PERPLEXING PYRAMID

Here's another **pyramid puzzle,** only this time it's even more mind-boggling! Fill in the pyramid so that a number appears in every empty cubie. Remember, numbers that appear in cubies **next to each other** must **add up to the number** in the one **directly above.**

Tip: Remember, start at the bottom and things will soon add up!

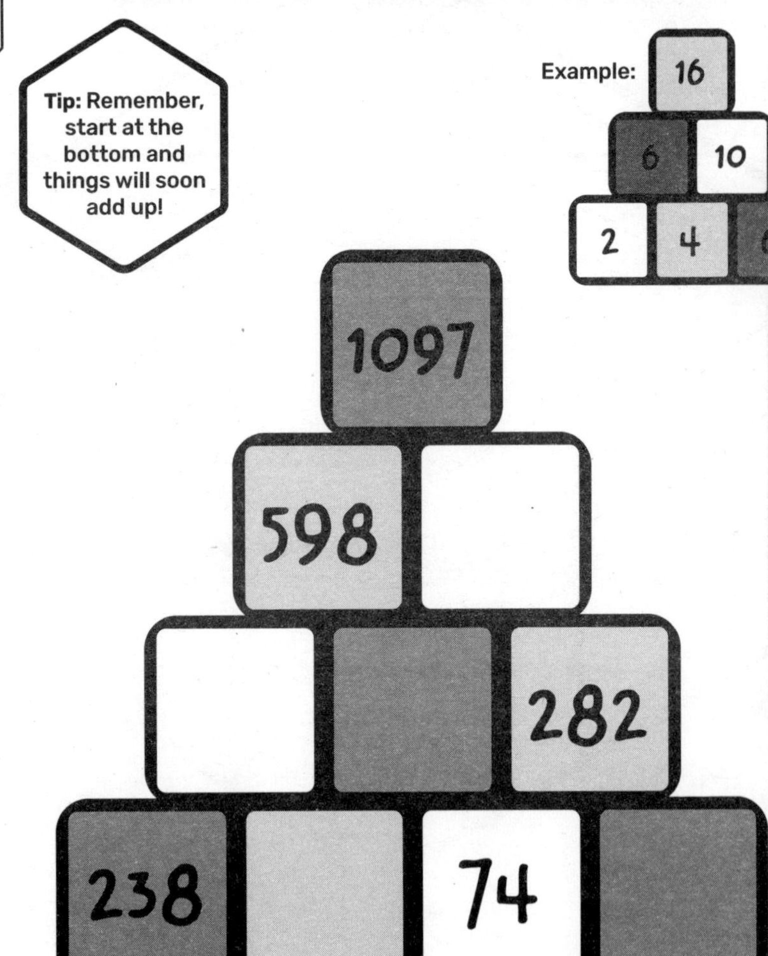

GAME OVER!

This final puzzle might just blow your mind! Make your way through the **twists and turns** of this **3D maze**, passing through three faces of this epic cube.

LEVEL 3

ANSWERS

6 CUBE COUNT

A
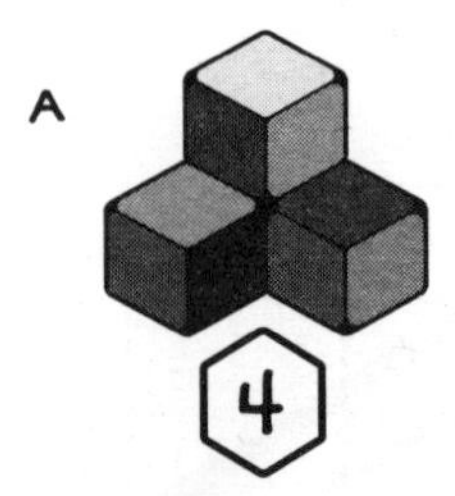
4

B
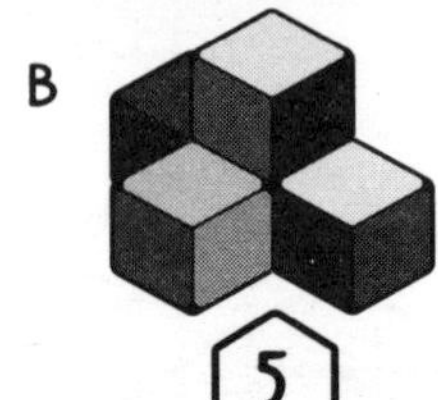
5

C
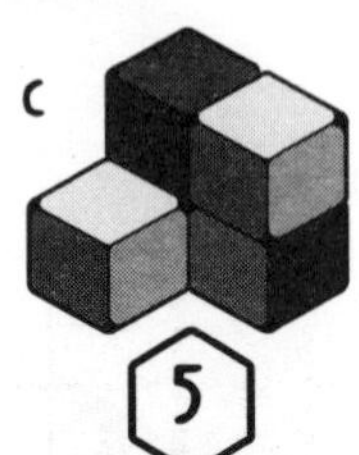
5

D

7

E
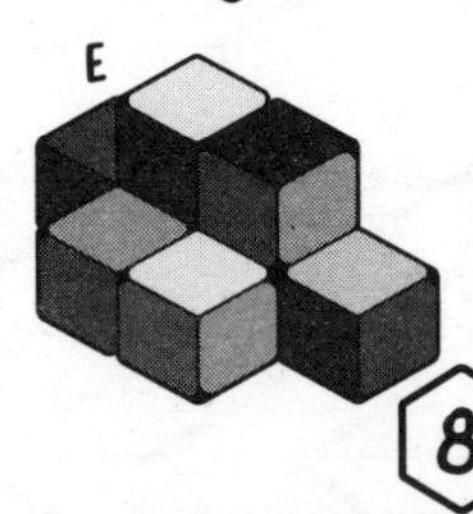
8

F
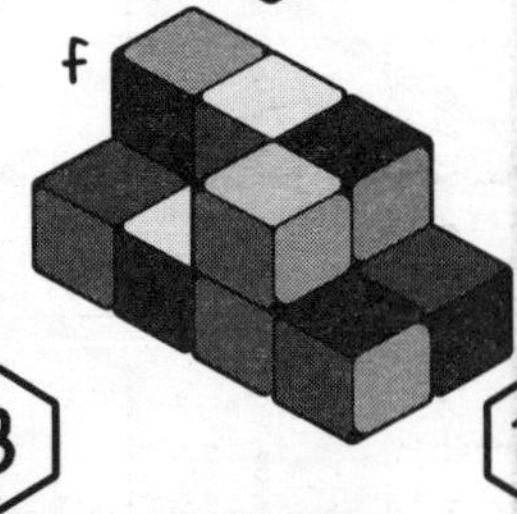
11

7 RUBIK'S LABYRINTH

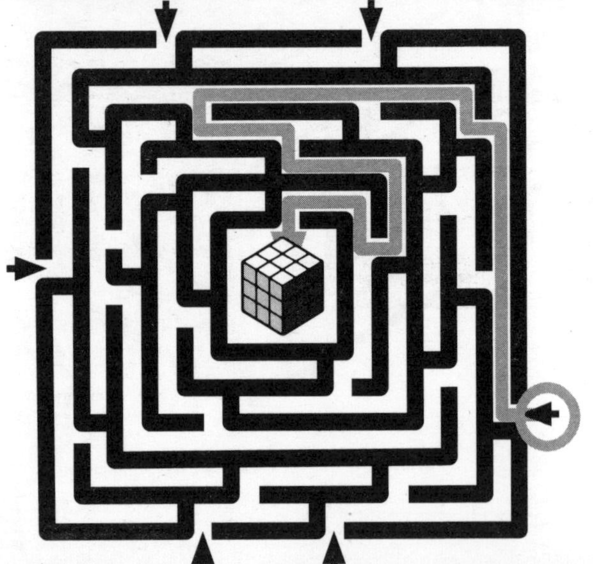

8 DOUBLE TROUBLE

PUZZLE 1

6	2	5	3	4	1
1	3	4	6	2	5
4	6	2	1	5	3
3	5	1	4	6	2
2	1	6	5	3	4
5	4	3	2	1	6

PUZZLE 2

1	4	6	5	2	3
6	2	4	3	1	5
5	3	1	2	6	4
2	1	3	4	5	6
4	5	2	6	3	1
3	6	5	1	4	2

PUZZLE 3

5	6	3	4	2	1
3	1	2	6	4	5
4	2	5	1	3	6
6	3	1	2	5	4
1	5	4	3	6	2
2	4	6	5	1	3

9 WHOSE CUBE?

C	U	B	E
C	U	T	E
M	U	T	E
M	I	T	E
M	I	N	E

10 CUBE CONUNDRUM

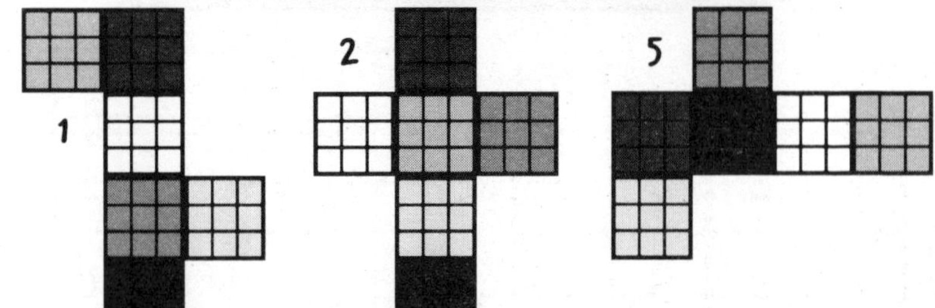

11 READY, SET, GO!

1

START >			A	M	J	R	U
N	D	C	B	C	N	O	M
F	E	J	K	L	M	B	E
G	H	I	A	U	N	O	T
I	F	U	L	W	E	P	L
L	D	C	S	T	A	Q	D
P	J	G	D	T	S	R	O
U	Y	W	V	U	B	Z	S
S	T	X	Y	Z	> FINISH		

2

START >			A	B	E	F	G
G	E	L	C	C	D	G	I
H	F	I	D	L	E	H	X
I	D	P	M	U	F	I	J
J	G	H	B	K	Q	U	K
T	R	S	Y	O	N	M	L
C	X	N	Q	P	P	S	C
N	T	S	R	Y	Z	T	Y
M	U	V	W	X	FINISH		

12 GRID GAMES

1

50	+	58	=	108
+		-		+
42	-	32	=	10
=		=		=
92	+	26	=	118

2

44	-	38	=	6
+		-		+
18	+	35	=	53
=		=		=
62	-	3	=	59

13 BEAT THE CUBE

PUZZLE 1
Easy

E	B	C	U
C	U	B	E
B	E	U	C
U	C	E	B

PUZZLE 2
Medium

C	U	E	B
B	E	C	U
E	B	U	C
U	C	B	E

14 WANNA PLAY?

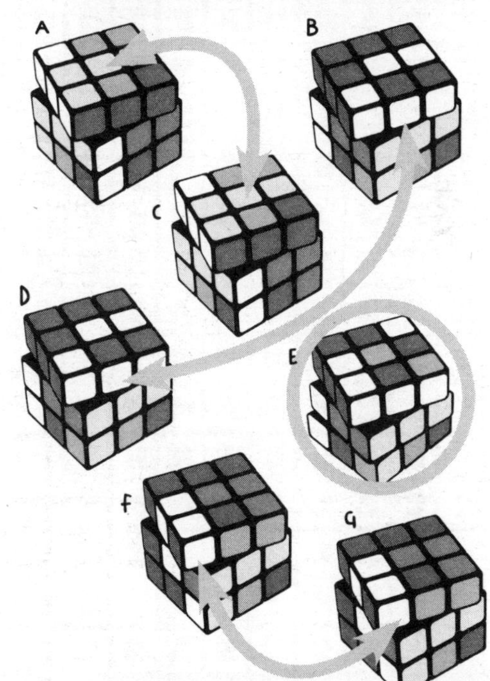

15 TWENTY IS PLENTY!

1	2	3	4	5
4	3	18	19	20
5	6	17	16	17
6	9	10	15	14
7	8	11	12	13

16 SEARCH AND SOLVE

V	R	H	R	J	O	C	M	Y	W	R	N	N	W	A
E	A	G	S	S	D	U	P	F	F	Q	O	I	Z	T
C	R	E	H	O	D	B	X	R	P	G	D	R	T	E
M	E	N	S	C	L	N	A	J	O	D	W	F	S	A
T	B	I	C	O	D	V	G	H	L	B	R	Z	I	S
H	U	U	R	J	J	O	E	O	P	F	L	M	W	E
I	C	S	A	W	L	B	N	Y	M	P	K	E	T	R
N	B	X	M	R	Y	I	J	A	T	L	O	G	M	S
K	Y	V	B	X	U	W	Y	B	Y	A	Z	B	Z	N
Z	Q	X	L	G	M	B	F	M	B	Y	E	O	R	R
P	A	P	E	A	L	B	I	G	N	E	P	W	P	U
J	P	U	Z	Z	L	E	B	K	A	R	D	N	R	T
V	S	W	S	P	E	E	D	O	S	M	V	B	D	A
M	P	O	H	F	M	T	Z	F	I	J	E	Q	Z	K
B	R	A	I	N	F	V	S	A	G	J	Z	R	T	W

17 RUBIK'S REBEL

18 DON'T MESS UP!

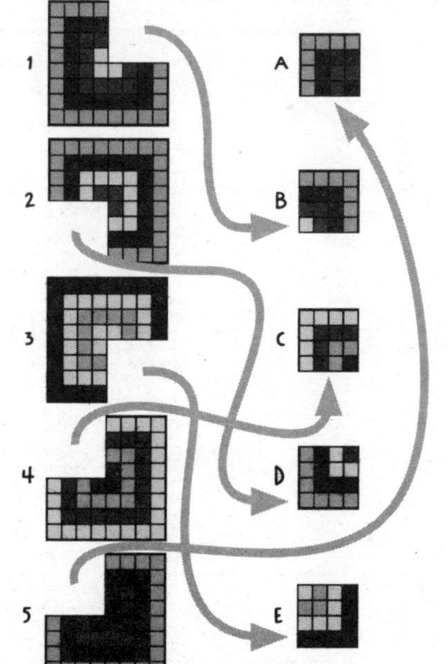

19 BRAINBUSTER

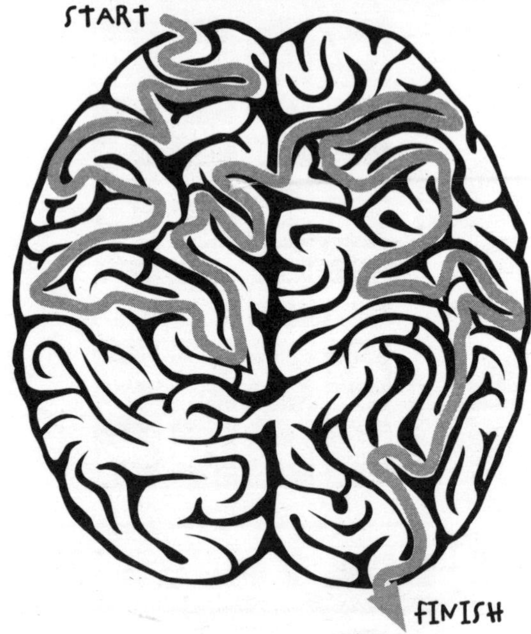

20 WORK OUT

1

2

3

4

21 #SPEEDSOLVING

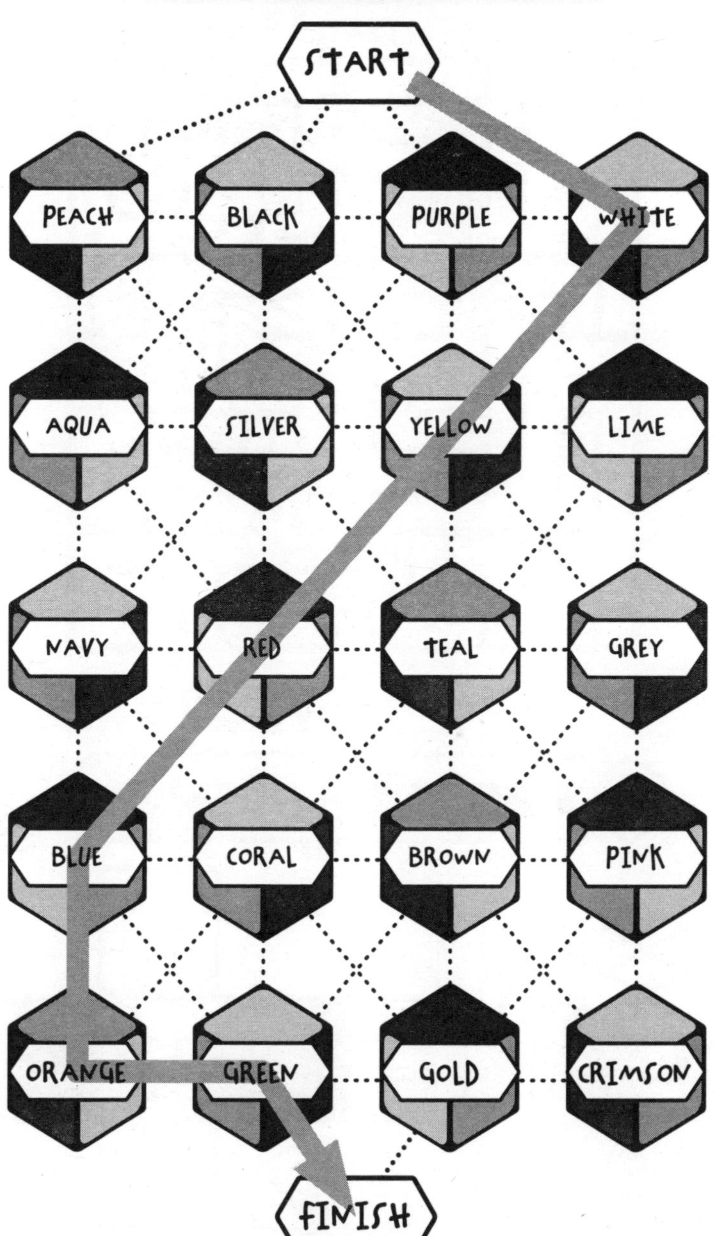

22 TWISTS AND TURNS

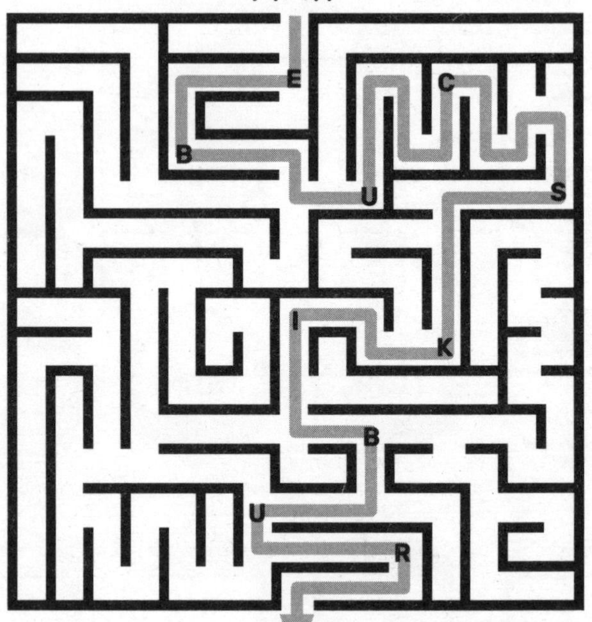

Answer: RUBIK'S CUBE

23 PROBLEM SOLVED

3

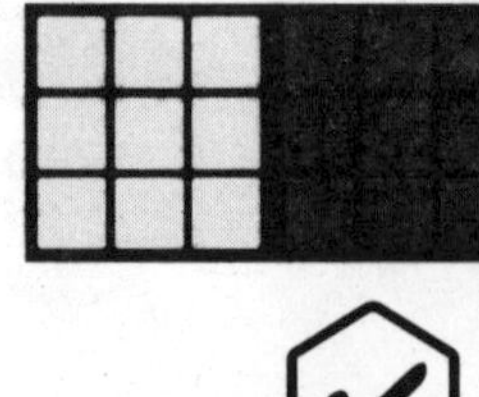

25 FUTOSHIKI FUN

PUZZLE 1

```
3   2   1 < 4
v           v
1   4   3   2
    v       ^
2   1   4 > 3
            v
4   3   2   1
```

PUZZLE 2

```
3 > 1 < 2   4
    ^   v
4   2   1   3
v
1   4   3   2
        ^
2   3 < 4 > 1
```

26 CODEBREAKER

A	B	C	D	E	F	G	H	I	J	K	L	M
26	25	24	23	22	21	20	19	18	17	16	15	14
N	**O**	**P**	**Q**	**R**	**S**	**T**	**U**	**V**	**W**	**X**	**Y**	**Z**
13	12	11	10	9	8	7	6	5	4	3	2	1

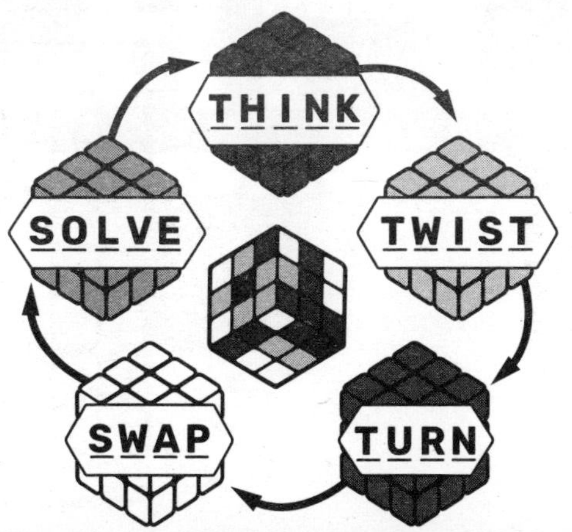

27 CUBE CONNECTION

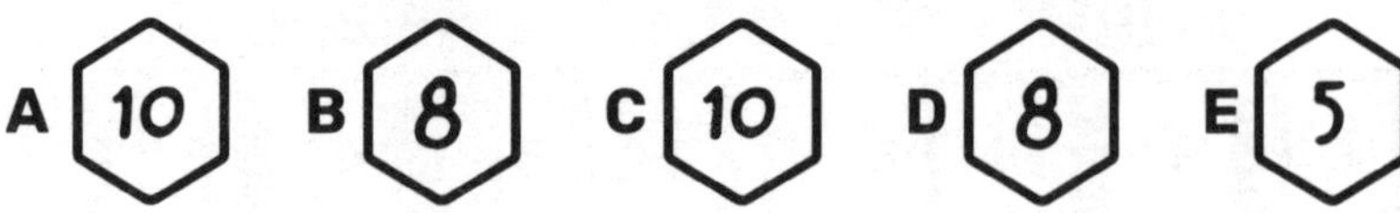

29 RUBIK'S REVEAL

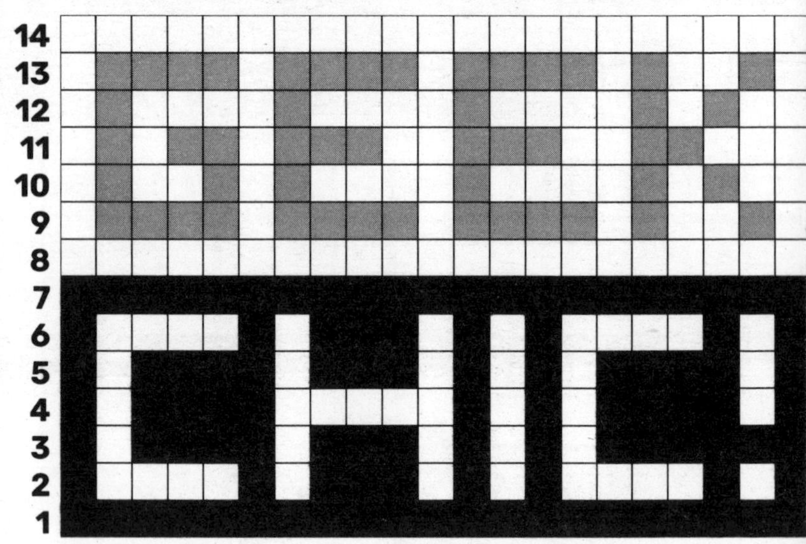

30 SHADING IT

PUZZLE 1

GREEN	BLUE	RED	YELLOW
YELLOW	RED	GREEN	BLUE
RED	YELLOW	BLUE	GREEN
BLUE	GREEN	YELLOW	RED

PUZZLE 2

BLUE	YELLOW	GREEN	RED
GREEN	RED	YELLOW	BLUE
RED	GREEN	BLUE	YELLOW
YELLOW	BLUE	RED	GREEN

31 VIEW FROM THE TOP

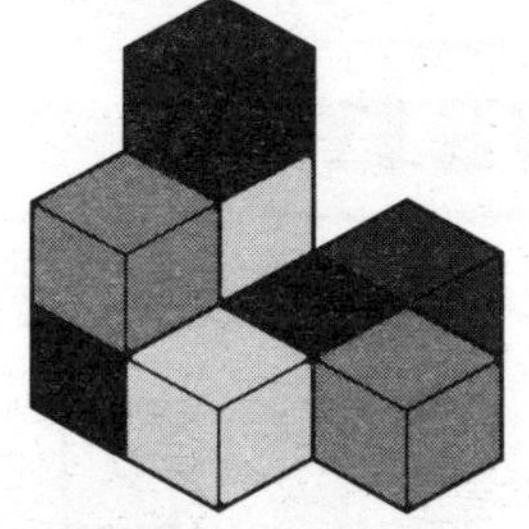

3

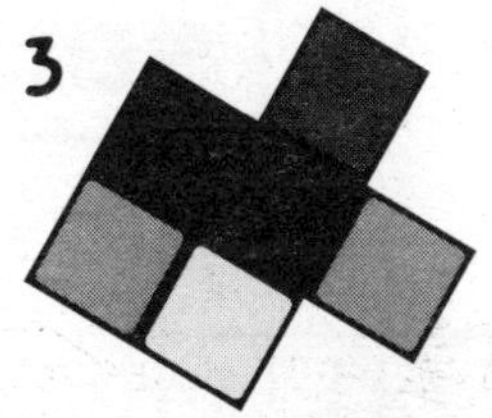

32 NINE INTO FOUR?

Here is one solution:

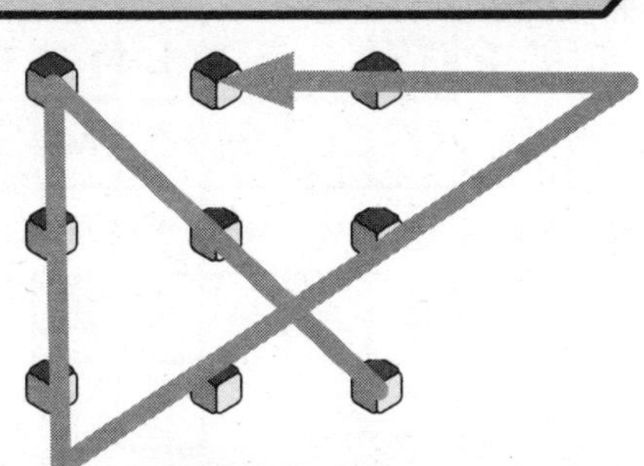

33 HIDDEN MESSAGE

COME TO THE NERD SIDE WE HAVE RUBIK'S CUBES!

34 OFF GRID

3 2 × 1 4 1 4 1

35 SOLVE IT!

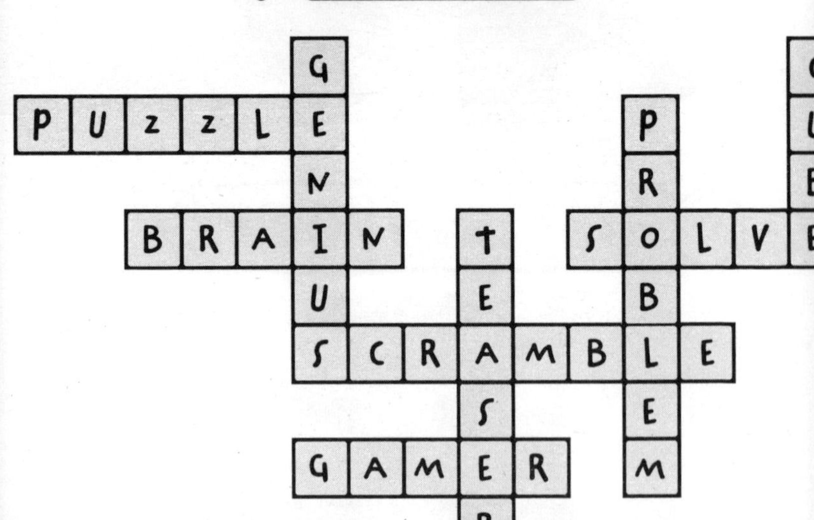

36 RUBIK'S RIDDLE

1 O	R	A	N	G	E			
	2 C	U	B	E				
		3 M	I	N	D			
	4 B	R	A	I	N			
	5 S	O	L	U	T	I	O	N
				6 S	P	E	E	D

The hidden word is:
GENIUS

37 AERIAL ACTION

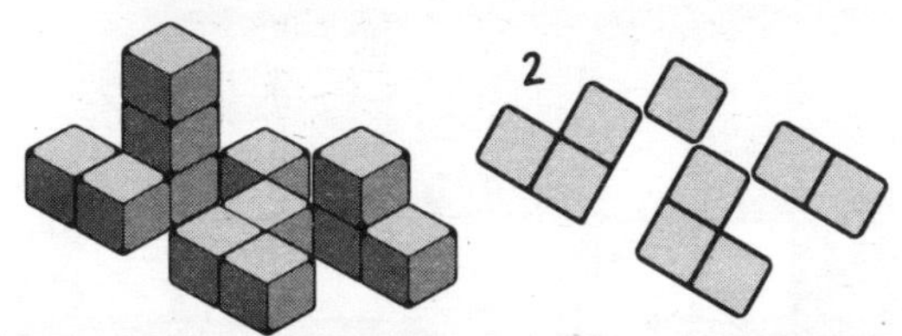

38 PYRAMID PUZZLER

39 TOTALLY TOUGH

5 + 8 + 3 = 16

14 + 12 + 6 = 32

14 + 12 + 11 = 37

40 LOVE TO PLAY

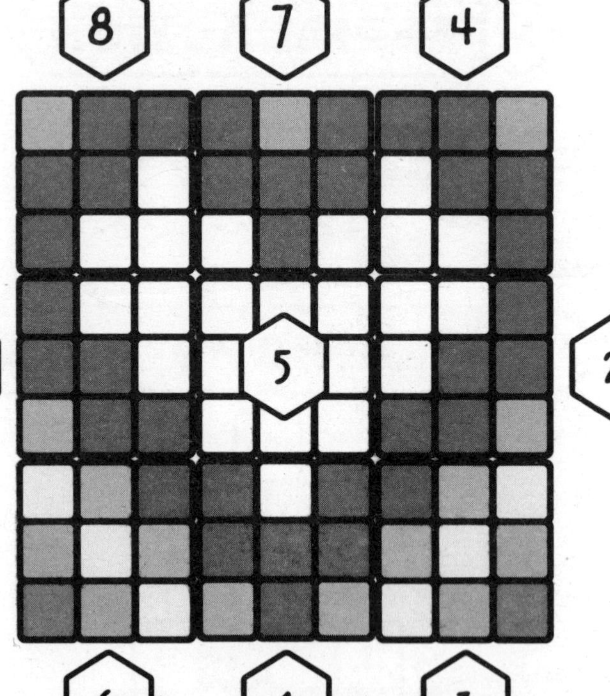

41 FIVE LIVES

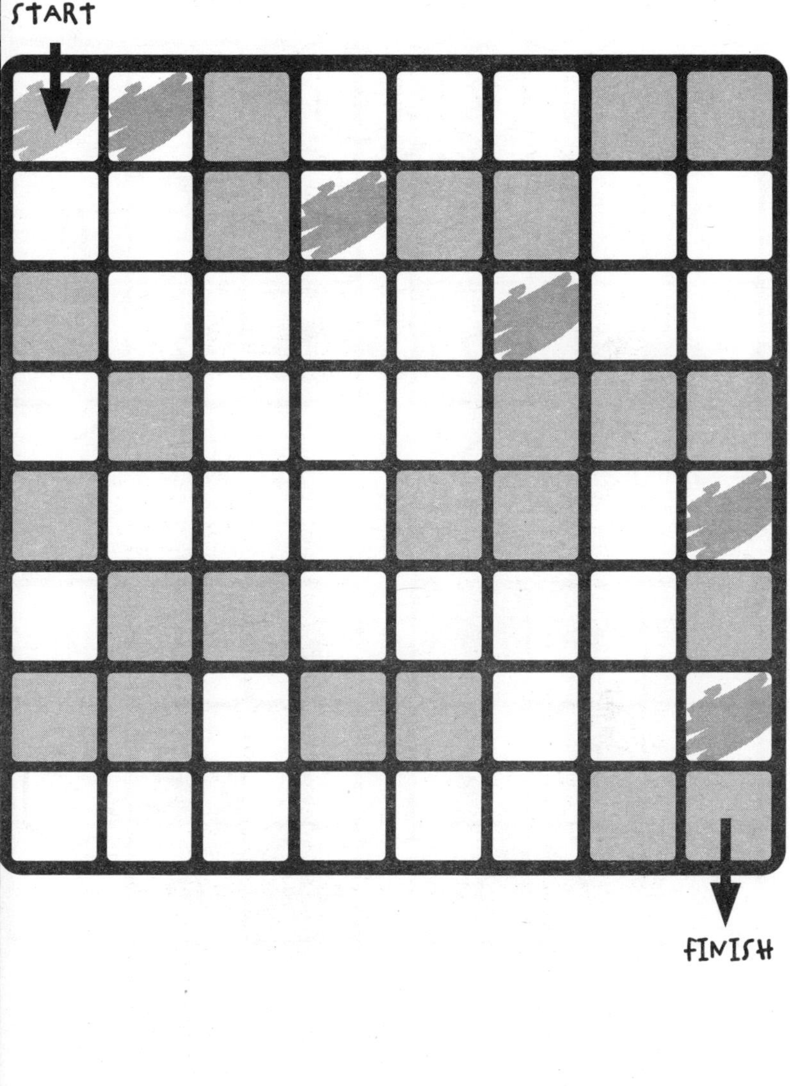

START

FINISH

42 MAGIC SQUARES

8	3	10
9	7	5
4	11	6

1. total = 21

7	14	9
12	10	8
11	6	13

2. total = 30

10	11	6
5	9	13
12	7	8

3. total = 27

18	8	10
4	12	20
14	16	6

4. total = 36

43 ALL SQUARE

4 x 4 squares = 1
3 x 3 squares = 4
2 x 2 squares = 9
1 x 1 squares = 16
Large middle squares = 2
Small middle squares = 8

TOTAL SQUARES:

44 UNIQUE CUBE

45 SQUARE EYES

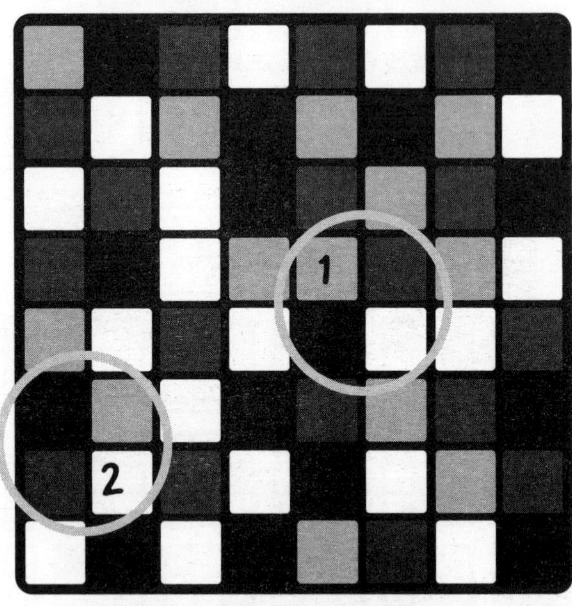

47 TOUGH TEST

PUZZLE 1

40	÷	20	=	2
x		÷		x
3	x	10	=	30
=		=		=
120	÷	2	=	60

PUZZLE 2

10	÷	5	=	2
x		x		x
24	÷	8	=	3
=		=		=
240	÷	40	=	6

48 PUZZLE PATH

1	2	3	5	19	21
2	8	6	7	10	20
3	4	5	8	23	24
12	11	10	9	22	23
13	16	17	18	21	24
14	15	20	19	20	25

49 NEXT LEVEL

1		3		2		4	<	5
^				v				
4		5		1		2	<	3
				^				
2		4	>	3		5		1
^				^				^
3		2		5		1		4
				v				
5	>	1		4	>	3		2

50 RUBIK'S RAINBOW

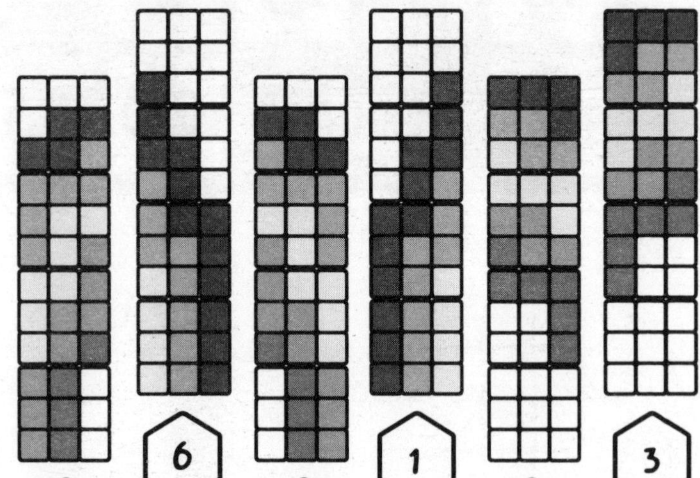

51 MASTER CUBE

A 6
B 7
C 9
D 8
E 13
F 6
G 7
H 13

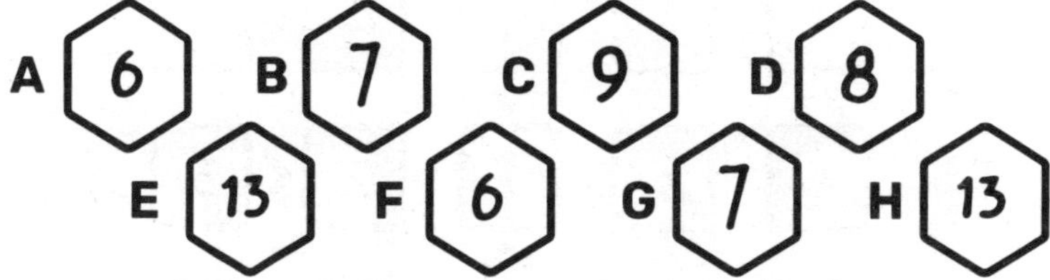

52 DARE TO PAIR

1
14
2
13
3
13
4
15
5
15
6
14

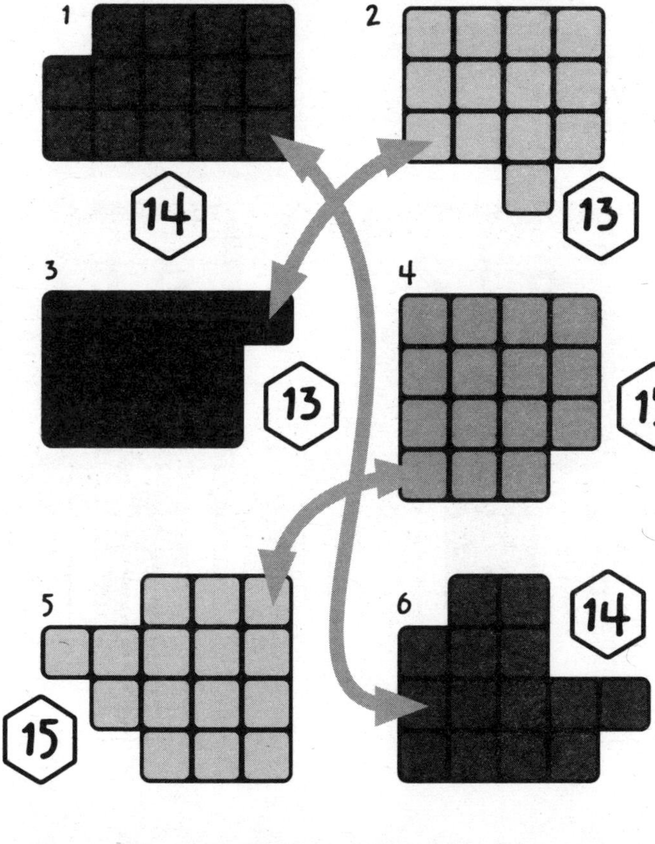

1

A + D = B + C

A = 2

2

C – B = A + D

B = 0

3

6	2
?	5

A – D = C – B

C = 3

4

A + B = C + D

D = 4

54 SHAPING UP

PUZZLE 1

5	1	2	3	4
2	3	4	5	1
4	5	1	2	3
3	4	5	1	2
1	2	3	4	5

PUZZLE 2

5	1	2	3	4
1	2	3	4	5
3	4	5	1	2
2	3	4	5	1
4	5	1	2	3

55 GAMER TAG

A	M	E	R	G
E	R	G	A	M
G	A	M	E	R
M	E	R	G	A
R	G	A	M	E

56 CUBE NUMBERS

A $1 \times 1 \times 1 =$ 1

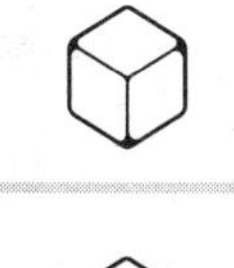

B $2 \times 2 \times 2 =$ 8

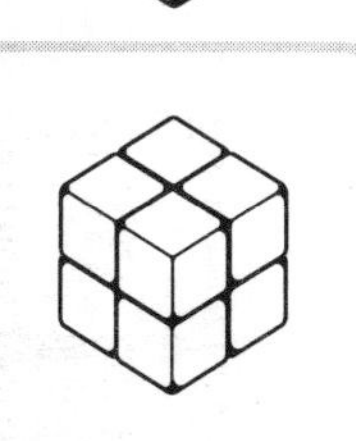

C $3 \times 3 \times 3 =$ 27

D $4 \times 4 \times 4 =$ 64

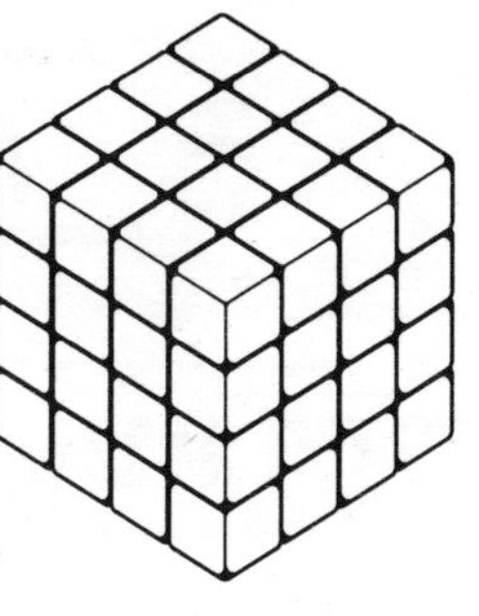

E $5 \times 5 \times 5 =$ 125

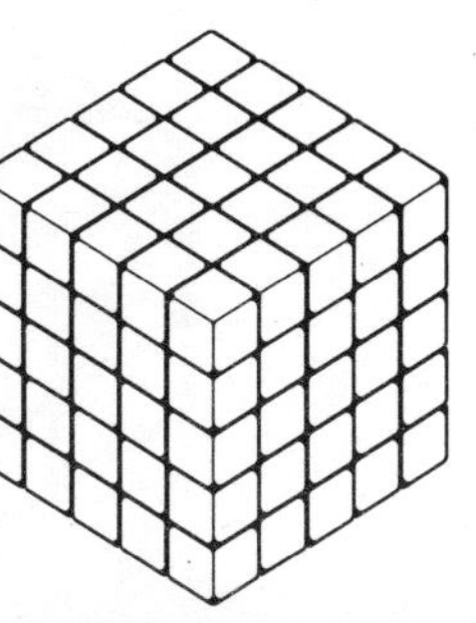

57 FACE VALUE

	2	3	4
+	2	3	4
+	2	3	4
=	7	0	2

59 A MULTITUDE OF CUBES!

25 ✔

These are some words you can make from the letters in RUBIK'S CUBE. You may spot others:

6 LETTERS:

BICKER, BIKERS, BRIBES, BRICKS, BRUISE, BUCKER, BUCKIE, BURIES, BURKES, BUSIER, BUSKER, CRUISE, CUBERS, CURIES, RUBIES, RUCKUS, SCRIBE, SICKER, SUBURB, SUCKER.

5 LETTERS:

BECKS, BERKS, BIKER, BIKES, BRIBE, BRICK, BRIES, BRISK, BUCKS, BURKS, CRIBS, CRICK, CRIES, CUBER, CUBES, CURBS, CURES, CURSE, ICERS, KERBS, KIBBE, REBUS, RICES, SCRUB, SKIER.

4 LETTERS:

BECK, BERK, BIBS, BIKE, BISK, BRIE, BUBS, BUCK, BURK, BUSK, CRIB, CUBE, CUBS, CUES, CURB, CURE, CURS, EBBS, ECRU, ICER, ICES, IRES, IRKS, KERB, RIBS, RICE, RICK, RISE, RISK, RUBS, RUCK, RUES, RUSE, RUSK, SICK, SIRE, SUCK, SURE, USER.

61 CUBER'S QUIZ

1. **True**
2. **True** – incredible!
3. **False** – six colours appear: white, yellow, red, blue, orange and green.
4. **True**
5. **True –** Californian Max Park set the fastest record – 3.13 seconds, on 11 June, 2023.
6. **False** – Ernő Rubik made his first cube puzzle in 1974.
7. **True**
8. **True!**

62 OVERVIEW

D

64 PERPLEXING PYRAMID

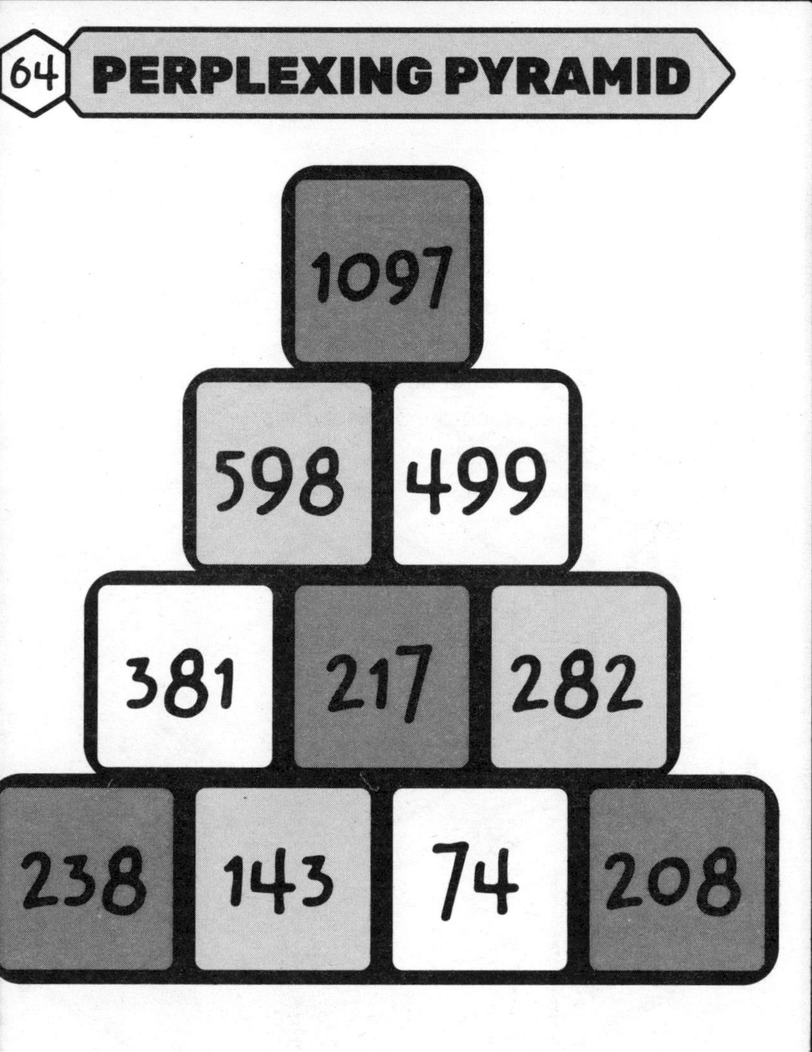

65 GAME OVER!